LANDMARK DECISIONS OF THE UNITED STATES SUPREME COURT VI

MAUREEN HARRISON & STEVE GILBERT
EDITORS

THE LANDMARK DECISIONS SERIES

EXCELLENT BOOKS
SAN DIEGO, CALIFORNIA

EXCELLENT BOOKS
Post Office Box 131322
Carlsbad, CA 92013-1322

Publisher's Cataloging in Publication Data

Landmark Decisions Of The United States Supreme Court VI/
    Maureen Harrison, Steve Gilbert, editors.
    p.   cm. - (Landmark Decisions Series)
Bibliography:p.
Includes Index.

1. United States. Supreme Court.
I. Title. II. Harrison, Maureen. III. Gilbert, Steve.
IV. Series: Landmark Decisions Series.

KF8742.H24 1999   LC 90-84578
347.'73'26-dc20
[347.3C726]
ISBN 1-880780-21-6

INTRODUCTION

Great are the old, few landmarks of the law.
They are the same in all times, and shall not be disturbed.
- Walt Whitman, Leaves Of Grass, 1860

Chiseled into the facade of the United States Supreme Court Building are these words:

EQUAL JUSTICE UNDER LAW

For many Americans seeking to redress a political wrong or vindicate a personal right, the search for "Equal Justice Under Law" has led to the United States Supreme Court. Justice Benjamin Cardozo wrote this about the people whose personal legal problems had reached the Supreme Court: *The sordid controversies of litigants are the stuff out of which great and shining truths will ultimately be shaped.* The "sordid controversies" of many ordinary, some famous, and a few infamous, individuals have all at one time or another found their way before the Supreme Court to become Justice Cardozo's "stuff out of which great and shining truths are shaped." These "truths," Supreme Court decisions, become binding legal precedents - the settled law of the land. The great nineteenth century observer of America, Alexis de Tocqueville, wrote in his 1835 study, *Democracy In America*: "When we have examined in detail the organization of the Supreme Court, and the entire prerogatives which it exercises, we shall readily admit that a more imposing judicial Power was never constituted by any people." The United States Supreme Court has exercised what de Tocqueville termed its "imposing judicial power" to settle all Constitutional controversies arising in the Federal Courts and all Constitutional questions arising in the State Courts since its creation in 1791.

In its long history, the Supreme Court has issued thousands of individual decisions. All have been important to the parties involved, but some, a significant few, have grown so important as to involve all Americans. These are Landmark Decisions, fundamentally altering the relationships of Americans to their institutions and to each other. Of these significant few, we have selected ten for inclusion in this book. These Landmark Decisions represent the great and continuing debates and controversies of American history and politics.

On the first Monday of each October the United States Supreme Court begins a new Term. From all over the country, on all kinds of issues, and for all kinds of reasons, Americans bring controversies to the Court for a final disposition. The Founding Fathers created the Supreme Court to construct and interpret the meaning of the Constitution. Chief Justice Charles Evans Hughes summed up the Court's responsibility in this way: "The Constitution is what the Judges say it is."

Every year over five thousand requests for review of lower court decisions are received by the Court. Requests, called *petitions for certiorari*, come to the Court from the losing side in Federal Appeals Courts or State Supreme Courts. Four of the nine Justices must agree to a review. Review is accepted in only about four hundred cases each year. Once accepted, written arguments - briefs, pro and con - are submitted to the Court by both the petitioner, the losing side appealing the lower court's decision against them, and the respondent, the winning side defending the lower court's decision for them. Interested parties, called *amici curiae*, friends of the Court, may be permitted to submit briefs in support of either side. After all submitted briefs are reviewed by the Justices, public oral arguments are heard by the Court. Ordinarily the opposing sides, the petitioner and the respondent, are given thirty minutes of oral argument. The Justices, at their discretion, may interrupt at any time to require further explanations, to pose hypothetical questions, or to make observations. Twice a week, on Wednesdays and Fridays, the Justices meet alone in conference to discuss each case and vote on its outcome. They may affirm [let stand] or reverse [change the outcome of] in whole or in part, the decisions of the lower courts from which these appeals have come. One Justice, voting in the majority, will be selected to write the majority opinion. Others may join in the majority opinion, write their own concurring opinion, write their own dissenting opinion, or join in another's concurrence or dissent. Drafts of the majority, concurring, and dissenting opinions circulate among the Justices, and are re-drafted and recirculated until a consensus is reached and a decision is announced. It is the majority opinion as finally issued by the Supreme Court that stands as the law of the land. All other Courts, Federal and State, are bound by Supreme Court precedent. The official legal texts of these decisions are published in the five hundred-plus volumes of *United States Reports*.

Judge Learned Hand wrote: "The language of the law must not be foreign to the ears of those who are to obey it." The ten Landmark Decisions presented in this book are carefully edited, plain-English versions of the official legal texts issued by the Supreme Court in *United States Reports*. We, as editors, have made every effort to replace esoteric legalese with understandable everyday English without damaging the original decisions. Edited out are long alpha-numeric legal citations and wordy wrangles over points of procedure. Edited in are definitions (*writ of habeas corpus* = an order from a judge to bring a person to court), translations (*certiorari* = the decision of the Court to review a case), identifications (petitioner = the individual appealing a lower court's decision; respondent = the individual defending the lower court's decision), and explanations (where the case originated, how it got to the court, and who all the parties involved were).

You will find in this book the majority opinion of the Court as expressed by the Justice chosen to speak for the Court. Preceding each edited decision, we note where the complete decision can be found. The bibliography provides a list of further reading on the cases and the Court. Also included for the reader's reference is a complete copy of the U.S. Constitution, to which every decision refers.

Chief Justice John Marshall wrote that a Supreme Court decision "comes home in its effects to every man's fire-side; it passes on his property, his reputation, his life, his all." We entered into editing *Landmark Decisions of the United States Supreme Court* because we, like you, and your family and friends, must obey, under penalty of law, these decisions. It stands to reason that, if we owe them our obedience, then we owe it to ourselves to know what they say, not second-hand, but for ourselves. We think it's time for you to have the final word.

M.H. & S.G.

TABLE OF CONTENTS

As there is no crime which can more excite and agitate the passions of men than treason, no charge demands more from the tribunal before which it is made a deliberate and temperate inquiry. Whether this inquiry be directed to the fact or to the law, none can be more solemn, none more important to the citizen or to the government; none can more affect the safety of both.

        - Chief Justice John Marshall (1807)

On the judges of this Court, then, is imposed the high and solemn duty of protecting, from even legislative violation, those contracts which the constitution of our country has placed beyond legislative control; and, however irksome the task may be, this is a duty from which we dare not shrink.   - Chief Justice John Marshall (1819)

As healthy mothers are essential to vigorous offspring, the physical well-being of woman becomes an object of public interest and care in order to preserve the strength and vigor of the race.

        - Justice David Brewer (1908)

Un-American Activities
"Are you now, or have you ever been, a member of the Communist Party?"
John T. Watkins v. United States
99

The [House Un-American Activities] Committee can radiate outward infinitely to any topic thought to be related in some way to armed insurrection. The outer reaches of this domain are known only by the content of "un-American activities."
— Chief Justice Earl Warren (1957)

There is no general privilege of silence. The First Amendment does not make speech or silence permissible to a person in such measure as he chooses. — Justice Tom Clark in dissent

One Person, One Vote
All Voters Are Created Equal
Reynolds v. Sims
137

The conception of political equality from the Declaration of Independence, to Lincoln's Gettysburg Address, to the Fifteenth, Seventeenth, and Nineteenth Amendments can mean only one thing - one person, one vote. — Chief Justice Earl Warren (1964)

The Constitution And The Right To Die
Physician-Assisted Suicide And The Law
Washington State v. Glucksberg
New York State v. Quill
153

The history of the law's treatment of assisted suicide in this country has been and continues to be one of the rejection of nearly all efforts to permit it. — Chief Justice William Rehnquist (1997)

Although the Constitution expressly authorizes the President to play a role in the process of enacting statutes, it is silent on the subject of unilateral Presidential action that either repeals or amends parts of duly enacted statutes.   - Justice John Paul Stevens (1998)

We the people of the United States, in order to form a more perfect union, establish justice, insure domestic tranquillity, provide for the common defense, promote the general welfare, and secure the blessings of liberty to ourselves and our posterity, do ordain and establish this Constitution for the United States of America.

The Aaron Burr Conspiracy
Was It Treason?
The Bollman-Swartwout Case

I, Thomas Jefferson, President of the United States . . . command all persons engaged in this unlawful enterprize [The Burr Conspiracy] to cease all further proceedings therein, as they will answer to the contrary at their own peril; and incur prosecution with all the rigors of law.

- President Jefferson's Proclamation, November 27, 1808

Treason against the United States shall consist only in levying war against them, or in adhering to their enemies, giving them aid and comfort.

- The Constitution's Treason Clause

On July 12, 1804, on New Jersey's Weehawken Heights, Vice President Aaron Burr fatally shot Treasury Secretary Alexander Hamilton. Burr escaped prosecution for the murder of Hamilton and served out his remaining term. Ex-Vice President Burr turned his political ambitions to the "Burr Conspiracy" - a scheme formed by him and General James Wilkinson, then Military Governor of the Louisiana Territory, to raise an Army, seize New Orleans, and use it as a base to "liberate" Mexico from Spain and/or the Western States and Territories from the United States.

On July 22, 1806 Burr sent two of his followers, Erick Bollman and Samuel Swartwout, each with a sealed copy of his plans, to General Wilkinson in New Orleans. Wilkerson, fearing the conspiracy had failed, and that he would soon be subject to President Jefferson's threatened "prosecution with all the rigors of law," double-crossed the pair. Bollman and Swartwout were arrested on charges of "treason in levying war against the United States."

Arguing that theirs had been no act of treason, as defined by the Constitution, Erick Bollman and Samuel Swartwout filed with the United States Supreme Court a writ of *habeas corpus* [an order to appear before a judge]. The Burr conspirators asked the Supreme Court to decide this question: "Was it treason?"

On February 21, 1807 the decision of the United States Supreme Court was announced by Chief Justice John Marshall.

The *Aaron Burr Conspiracy* Court

Chief Justice John Marshall
Appointed Chief Justice by President John Adams
Served 1801 - 1835

Associate Justice William Cushing
Appointed by President Washington
Served 1789 - 1810

Associate Justice Samuel Chase
Appointed by President Washington
Served 1796 - 1811

Associate Justice Bushrod Washington
Appointed by President John Adams
Served 1798 - 1829

Associate Justice William Johnson
Appointed by President Jefferson
Served 1804 - 1834

Associate Justice Henry Livingston
Appointed by President Jefferson
Served 1806 - 1823

The unedited legal text of *In The Matter of Bollman and Swartwout* can be found in volume 8 of *United States Reports* beginning on page 75. Our edited plain-English text follows.

The Aaron Burr Conspiracy
February 21, 1807

Chief Justice John Marshall: The prisoners having been brought before this court on a writ of habeas corpus [an order to appear before a judge], and the testimony on which they were committed having been fully examined and attentively considered, the court is now to declare the law upon their case.

This being a mere inquiry, which, without deciding upon guilt, precedes the institution of a prosecution, the question to be determined is, whether the accused shall be discharged or held to trial, and if the latter, in what place they are to be tried, and whether they shall be confined or admitted to bail. "If," says a very learned and accurate commentator, "upon this inquiry it manifestly appears that no such crime has been committed, or that the suspicion entertained of the prisoner was wholly groundless, in such cases only is it lawful totally to discharge him. Otherwise he must either be committed to prison or give bail."

The specific charge brought against the prisoners is treason in levying war against the United States.

As there is no crime which can more excite and agitate the passions of men than treason, no charge demands more from the tribunal before which it is made a deliberate and temperate inquiry. Whether this inquiry be directed to the fact or to the law, none can be more solemn, none more important to the citizen or to the government; none can more affect the safety of both.

To prevent the possibility of those calamities which result from the extension of treason to offenses of minor importance, that great fundamental law which defines and limits the various departments of our government has given a rule on the subject both to the legislature and the courts of America, which neither can be permitted to transcend.

"Treason against the United States: shall consist only in levying war against them, or in adhering to their enemies, giving them aid and comfort."

To constitute that specific crime for which the prisoners now before the court have been committed, war must be actually levied against the United States. However flagitious may be the crime of conspiring to subvert by force the government of our country, such conspiracy is not treason. To conspire to levy war, and actually to levy war, are distinct offenses. The first must be brought into operation by the assemblage of men for a purpose treasonable in itself, or the fact of levying war cannot have been committed. So far has this principle been carried, that, in a case reported by Ventris, and mentioned in some modern treatises on criminal law, it has been determined that the actual enlistment of men to serve against the government does not amount to levying war. It is true that in that case the soldiers enlisted were to serve without the realm, but they were enlisted within it, and if the enlistment for a treasonable purpose could amount to levying war, then war had been actually levied.

It is not the intention of the court to say that no individual can be guilty of this crime who has not appeared in arms against his country. On the contrary, if war be actually levied, that is, if a body of men be actually assembled for the purpose of effecting by force a treasonable purpose, all those who perform any part, however minute, or however remote from the scene of action, and who are actually leagued in the general conspiracy, are to be considered as traitors. But there must be an actual assembling of men for the treasonable purpose to constitute a levying of war.

Crimes so atrocious as those which have for their object the subversion by violence of those laws and those institutions which have been ordained in order to secure the peace and happiness of society, are not to escape punishment because they have not ripened into treason. The wisdom of the legislature is competent to provide for the case; and the framers of our constitution, who not only defined and limited the crime, but with jealous circumspection attempted to protect their limitation by providing that no person should be convicted of it, unless on the testimony of two witnesses to the same overt act, or on confession in open court, must have conceived it more safe that punishment in such cases should be ordained by general laws, formed upon deliberation, under the influence of no resentments and without knowing on whom they were to operate, than that it should be inflicted under the influence of those passions which the occasion seldom fails to excite, and which a flexible definition of the crime, or a construction which would render it flexible, might bring into operation. It is therefore more safe as well as more consonant to the principles of our constitution, that the crime of treason should not be extended by construction to doubtful cases, and that crimes not clearly within the constitutional definition should receive such punishment as the legislature in its wisdom may provide.

To complete the crime of levying war against the United States, there must be an actual assemblage of men for the purpose of executing a treasonable design. In the case now before the court, a design to overturn the government of the United States in New Orleans by force would have been unquestionably a design which, if carried into execution, would have been treason, and the assemblage of a body of men for the purpose of carrying it into execution would amount to levying of war against the United States; but no conspiracy for this object, no enlisting of men to effect it, would be an actual levying of war.

In conformity with the principles now laid down have been the decisions heretofore made by the judges of the United States.

The opinions given by Judge Paterson and Judge Iredell, in cases before them, imply an actual assembling of men, though they rather designed to remark on the purpose to which the force was to be applied than on the nature of the force itself. Their opinions, however, contemplate the actual employment of force.

Judge Chase, in the trial of Fries, was more explicit. He stated the opinion of the court to be, "that if a body of people conspire and meditate an insurrection to resist or oppose the execution of any statute of the United States by force, they are only guilty of a high misdemeanor; but if they proceed to carry such intention into execution by force, that they are guilty of the treason of levying war; and the quantum of the force employed neither lessens nor increases the crime; whether by one hundred, or one thousand persons, is wholly immaterial." "The court are of the opinion," continued Judge Chase, on that occasion, "that a combination or conspiracy to levy war against the United States is not treason, unless combined with an attempt to carry such combination or conspiracy into execution; some actual force or violence must be used in pursuance of such design to levy war; but it is altogether immaterial whether the force used is sufficient to effectuate the object; any force connected with the intention will constitute the crime of levying war."

The application of these general principles to the particular case before the court will depend on the testimony which has been exhibited against the accused.

The first deposition [sworn testimony] to be considered is that of General Eaton. This gentleman connects in one statement the purport of numerous conversations held with Colonel Burr throughout the last winter. In the course of these conversations were communicated various criminal projects which seem to have been revolving in the mind of the projector. An expedition against Mexico seems to have been the first and most matured part of his plan, if indeed it did not constitute a distinct and separate plan, upon the success of which other schemes still more culpable, but not yet well digested, might depend. Maps and other information preparatory to its execution, and which would rather indicate that it was the immediate object, had been procured, and for a considerable time, in repeated conversations, the whole efforts of Colonel Burr were directed to prove to the witness, who was to have held a high command under him, the practicability of the enterprise, and in explaining to him the means by which it was to be effected.

This deposition exhibits the various schemes of Colonel Burr, and its materiality depends on connecting the prisoners at the bar in such of those schemes as were treasonable. For this purpose the affidavit [written statement of facts, sworn to by its author] of General Wilkinson, comprehending in its body the substance of a letter from Colonel Burr, has been offered, and was received by the circuit court. To the admission of this testimony great and serious objections have been made. It has been urged that it is a voluntary or rather an extra-judicial affidavit, made before a person not appearing to be a magistrate, and contains the substance only of a letter, of which the original is retained by the person who made the affidavit.

The objection that the affidavit is extra-judicial resolves itself into the question whether one magistrate may commit on an affidavit taken before another magistrate. For if he may, an affidavit made as the foundation of a commitment ceases to be extra-judicial, and the person who makes it would be as liable to a prosecution for perjury as if the warrant of commitment had been issued by the magistrate before whom the affidavit was made.

To decide that an affidavit made before one magistrate would not justify a commitment by another, might in many cases be productive of great inconvenience, and does not appear susceptible of abuse if the verity of the certificate be established. Such an affidavit seems admissible on the principle that before the accused is put upon his trial all the proceedings are ex parte [one-sided]. The court therefore overrule this objection.

That which questions the character of the person who has on this occasion administered the oath is next to be considered.

The certificate from the office of the department of state has been deemed insufficient by the counsel for the prisoners, because the law does not require the appointment of magistrates for the territory of New Orleans to be certified to that office, because the certificate is in itself informal, and because it does not appear that the magistrate had taken the oath required by the act of congress.

The first of these objections is not supported by the law of the case, and the second may be so readily corrected, that the court has proceeded to consider the subject as if it were corrected, retaining however any final decision, if against the prisoners, until the correction shall be made. With regard to the third, the magistrate must be presumed to have taken the requisite oaths, since he is found acting as a magistrate.

On the admissibility of that part of the affidavit which purports to be as near the substance of the letter from Colonel Burr to General Wilkinson as the latter could interpret it, a division of opinion has taken place in the court. Two judges are of opinion that as such testimony delivered in the presence of the prisoner on his trial would be totally inadmissible, neither can it be considered as a foundation for a commitment. Although in making a commitment the magistrate does not decide on the guilt of the prisoner, yet he does decide on the probable cause, and a long and painful imprisonment may be the consequence of his decision. This probable cause, therefore, ought to be proved by testimony in itself legal, and which, though from the nature of the case it must be ex parte, ought in many other respects to be such as a court and jury might hear.

Two judges are of opinion that in this incipient stage of the prosecution an affidavit stating the general purport of a letter may be read, particularly where the person in possession of it is at too great a distance to admit of its being obtained, and that a commitment may be founded on it.

Under this embarrassment it was deemed necessary to look into the affidavit for the purpose of discovering whether, if admitted, it contains matter which would justify the commitment of the prisoners at the bar on the charge of treason.

That the letter from Colonel Burr to General Wilkinson relates to a military enterprise meditated by the former, has not been questioned. If this enterprise was against Mexico, it would amount to a high misdemeanor; if against any of the territories of the United States, or if in its progress the subversion of the government of the United States in any of their territories was a mean clearly and necessarily to be employed, if such mean formed a substantive part of the plan, the assemblage of a body of men to effect it would be levying war against the United States.

The letter is in language which furnishes no distinct view of the design of the writer. The cooperation, however, which is stated to have been secured, points strongly to some expedition against the territories of Spain. After making these general statements, the writer becomes rather more explicit, and says, "Burr's plan of operations is to move down rapidly from the falls on the 15th of November with the first 500 or 1,000 men in light boats now constructing for that purpose, to be at Natchez between the 5th and 15th of December, there to meet Wilkinson, then to determine whether it will be expedient in the first instance to seize on or to pass by Baton Rouge. The people of the country to which we are going are prepared to receive us. Their agents now with Burr say that if we will protect their religion, and will not subject them to a foreign power, in three weeks all will be settled."

There is no expression in these sentences which would justify a suspicion that any territory of the United States was the object of the expedition.

For what purpose seize on Baton Rouge; why engage Spain against this enterprise, if it was designed against the United States?

"The people of the country to which we are going are prepared to receive us." This language is peculiarly appropriate to a foreign country. It will not be contended that the terms would be inapplicable to a territory of the United States; but other terms would more aptly convey the idea, and Burr seems to consider himself as giving information of which Wilkinson was not possessed. When it is recollected that he was the governor of a territory adjoining that which must have been threatened, if a territory of the United States was threatened, and that he commanded the army, a part of which was stationed in that territory, the probability that the information communicated related to a foreign country, it must be admitted, gains strength.

"Their agents now with Burr say that if we will protect their religion, and will not subject them to a foreign power, in three weeks all will be settled." This is apparently the language of a people who, from the contemplated change in their political situation, feared for their religion, and feared that they would be made the subjects a foreign power. That the Mexicans should entertain these apprehensions was natural, and would readily be believed. They were, if the representation made of their dispositions be correct, about to place themselves much in the power of men who professed a different faith from theirs, and who, by making them dependent on England or the United States, would subject them to a foreign power. That the people of New Orleans, as a people, if really engaged in the conspiracy, should feel the same apprehensions, and require assurances on the same points, is by no means so obvious.

There certainly is not in the letter delivered to General Wilkinson, so far as that letter is laid before the court, one syllable which has a necessary or a natural reference to an enterprise against any territory of the United States. That the bearer of the letter must be considered as acquainted with its contents is not to be controverted. The letter and his own declarations evince the fact.

After stating himself to have passed through New York, and the western states and territories, without insinuating that he had performed on his route any act whatever which was connected with the enterprise, he states their object to be, "to carry an expedition into the Mexican provinces." This statement may be considered as explanatory of the letter of Colonel Burr, if the expressions of that letter could be thought ambiguous.

But there are other declarations made by Mr. Swartwout, which constitute the difficulty of this case. On an inquiry from General Wilkinson, he said, "this territory would be revolutionized where the people were ready to join them, and that there would be some seizing, he supposed, at New Orleans." If these words import that the government established by the United States in any of its territories, was to be revolutionized by force, although merely as a step to, or a mean of executing some greater projects, the design was unquestionably treasonable, and any assemblage of men for that purpose would amount to a levying of war. But on the import of the words a difference of opinion exists. Some of the judges suppose they refer to the territory against which the expedition was intended, others to that in which the conversation was held. Some consider the words, if even applicable to a territory at the United States, as alluding to a revolution to be effected by the people, rather than by the party conducted by Colonel Burr.

But whether this treasonable intention be really imputable to the plan or not, it is admitted that it must have been carried into execution by an open assemblage of men for that purpose, previous to the arrest of the prisoner, in order to consummate the crime as to him; and a majority of the court is of opinion that the conversation of Mr. Swartwout affords no sufficient proof of such assembling.

The prisoner stated that "Colonel Burr, with the support of a powerful association extending from New York to New Orleans, was levying an armed body of 7,000 men from the state of New York and the western states and territories, with a view to carry an expedition to the Mexican territories." That the association, whatever may be its purpose, is not treason, has been already stated. That levying an army may or may not be treason, and that this depends on the intention with which it is levied, and on the point to which the parties have advanced, has been also stated. The mere enlisting of men, without assembling them, is not levying war. The question then is whether this evidence proves

Colonel Burr to have advanced so far in levying an army as actually to have assembled them.

It is argued that since it cannot be necessary that the whole 7,000 men should have assembled, their commencing their march by detachments to the place of rendezvous must be sufficient to constitute the crime. This position is correct, with some qualification. It cannot be necessary that the whole army should assemble, and that the various parts which are to compose it should have combined. But it is necessary that there should be an actual assemblage, and therefore the evidence should make the fact unequivocal. The traveling of individuals to the place of rendezvous would perhaps not be sufficient. This would be an equivocal act, and has no warlike appearance. The meeting of particular bodies of men, and their marching from places of partial to a place of general rendezvous, would be such an assemblage.

The particular words used by Mr. Swartwout are, that Colonel Burr "was levying an armed body of 7,000 men." If the term *levying* in this place imports that they were assembled, then such fact would amount, if the intention be against the United States, to levying war. If it barely imports that he was enlisting or engaging them in his service, the fact would not amount to levying war.

It is thought sufficiently apparent that the latter is the sense in which the term was used. The fact alluded to, if taken in the former sense, is of a nature so to force itself upon the public view, that if the army had then actually assembled, either together or in detachments, some evidence of such assembling would have been laid before the court.

The words used by the prisoner in reference to seizing at New Orleans, and borrowing perhaps by force from the bank, though indicating a design to rob, and consequently importing a high offense, do not designate the specific crime of levying war against the United States.

It is therefore the opinion of a majority of the court, that in the case of Samuel Swartwout there is not sufficient evidence of his levying war against the United States to justify his commitment on the charge of treason.

Against Erick Bollman there is still less testimony. Nothing has been said by him to support the charge that the enterprise in which he was engaged had any other object than was stated in the letter of Colonel Burr. Against him, therefore, there is no evidence to support a charge of treason.

That both of the prisoners were engaged in a most culpable enterprise against the dominions of a power at peace with the United States, those who admit the affidavit of General Wilkinson cannot doubt. But that no part of this crime was committed in the District of Columbia is apparent. It is therefore the unanimous opinion of the court that they cannot be tried in this district.

The law read on the part of the prosecution is understood to apply only to offenses committed on the high seas, or in any river, haven, basin or bay not within the jurisdiction of any particular state. In those cases there is no court which has particular cognizance of the crime, and therefore the place in which the criminal shall be apprehended, or, if he be apprehended where no court has exclusive jurisdiction, that to which he shall be first brought, is substituted for the place in which the offense was committed.

But in this case, a tribunal for the trial of the offense, wherever it may have been committed, had been provided by Congress; and at the place where the prisoners were seized by the authority of the commander-in-chief, there existed such a tribunal. It would, too, be extremely dangerous to say that because the prisoners were apprehended, not by a civil magistrate, but by the military power, there could be given by law a right to try the persons so seized in any place which the general might select, and to which he might direct them to be carried.

The act of Congress which the prisoners are supposed to have violated, describes as offenders those who begin or set on foot, or provide, or prepare, the means for any military expedition or enterprise to be carried on from thence against the dominions of a foreign prince or state, with whom the United States are at peace.

There is a want of precision in the description of the offense which might produce some difficulty in deciding what cases would come within it. But several other questions arise which a court consisting of four judges finds itself unable to decide, and therefore, as the crime with which the prisoners stand charged has not been committed, the court can only direct them to be discharged. This is done with the less reluctance because the discharge does not acquit [release] them from the offense which there is probable cause for supposing they have committed, and if those whose duty it is to protect the nation, by prosecuting offenders against the laws, shall suppose those who have been charged with treason to be proper objects for punishment, they will, when possessed of less exceptionable testimony, and when able to say at what place the offense has been committed, institute fresh proceedings against them.

The Dartmouth College Case
Daniel Webster Defends His Alma Mater
The Trustees of Dartmouth College v. Woodward

No State shall pass any law impairing the obligation of contracts.
- The U.S. Constitution's Contract Clause

In 1769 England's King George III granted a Royal Charter for the establishment of a private New England college to be named after the Earl of Dartmouth.

On June 27, 1816 the New Hampshire Legislature enacted a law seizing public control of the private Dartmouth College. The ousted Trustees retained Dartmouth graduate Daniel Webster, Class of 1801, to represent them. Webster, arguing that the Dartmouth Charter was a private contract protected from state interference under the U.S. Constitution's Contract Clause, filed suit in the New Hampshire Courts against Dartmouth's new state-appointed Treasurer, William Woodward. On November 6, 1816 New Hampshire's Superior Court of Appeals found for Woodward. The Trustees appealed to the United States Supreme Court.

Oral arguments were heard on March 10, 1818 and Webster concluded his legal argument with this summation: *This, sir, is my case. It is the case, not merely of that humble institution, it is the case of every college in our land. It is more. It is the case of every eleemosynary institution throughout our country, of all those great charities founded by the piety of our ancestors to alleviate human misery, and scatter blessings along the pathway of human life. It is more. It is, in some sense, the case of every man who has property of which he may be stripped, - for the question is simply this: Shall our state legislature be allowed to take that which is not their own, to turn it from its original use, and apply it to such ends or purposes as they, in their discretion, shall see fit? Sir, you may destroy this little institution; it is weak; it is in your hands! You may put it out; but if you do, you must carry on your work! You must extinguish, one after another, all those great lights of science, which, for more than a century, have thrown their radiance over the land! It is, sir, as I have said, a small college, - and yet there are those who love it. . . .*

On February 2, 1819 the 5-1 decision of the United States Supreme Court was announced by Chief Justice John Marshall.

The *Dartmouth College* Court

Chief Justice John Marshall
Appointed Chief Justice by President John Adams
Served 1801 - 1835

Associate Justice Bushrod Washington
Appointed by President John Adams
Served 1798 - 1829

Associate Justice William Johnson
Appointed by President Jefferson
Served 1804 - 1834

Associate Justice Henry Livingston
Appointed by President Jefferson
Served 1806 - 1823

Associate Justice Joseph Story
Appointed by President Madison
Served 1811 - 1845

Associate Justice Gabriel Duvall
Appointed by President Madison
Served 1811 - 1834

The unedited legal text of *The Trustees of Dartmouth College v. Woodward* can be found in volume 17 of *United States Reports* beginning on page 518. Our edited plain-English text follows.

The Trustees Of Dartmouth College
v. Woodward
February 2, 1819

Chief Justice John Marshall: This is an action [a suit] . . . brought by the Trustees of Dartmouth College against William H. Woodward, in the State Court of New Hampshire, for [possession of] the book of records, corporate seal, and other corporate property, to which [Dartmouth alleges itself] to be entitled.

A special verdict . . . finds for the defendant [Woodward], if certain acts of the legislature of New Hampshire, passed on the 27th of June, and on the 18th of December, 1816, be valid, and binding on the trustees without their assent, and not repugnant to the Constitution of the United States; otherwise, it finds for the plaintiffs [Dartmouth].

The Superior Court of Judicature of New Hampshire rendered a judgment upon this verdict for [Woodward], which judgment has been brought before this Court. . . . The single question now to be considered is: do the acts to which the verdict refers violate the Constitution of the United States?

This Court can be insensible neither to the magnitude nor delicacy of this question. The validity of a legislative act is to be examined; and the opinion of the highest law tribunal of a State is to be revised, an opinion which carries with it intrinsic evidence of the diligence, of the ability, and the integrity, with which it was formed. On more than one occasion, this Court has expressed the cautious circumspection with which it approaches the consideration of such questions; and has declared that in no doubtful case would it pronounce a legislative act to be contrary to the Constitution. But the American people have said, in the Constitution of the United States, that "no State shall pass any bill

of attainder, ex post facto law, or law impairing the obligation of contracts." In the same instrument they have also
said, "that the judicial power shall extend to all cases in law
and equity [fairness] arising under the Constitution." On the
judges of this Court, then, is imposed the high and solemn
duty of protecting, from even legislative violation, those
contracts which the Constitution of our country has placed
beyond legislative control; and, however irksome the task
may be, this is a duty from which we dare not shrink.

The title of [Dartmouth] originates in a charter dated the
13th day of December, in the year 1769, incorporating
twelve persons therein mentioned, by the name of "The
Trustees of Dartmouth College," granting to them and
their successors the usual corporate privileges and powers,
and authorizing the trustees, who are to govern the college,
to fill up all vacancies which may be created in their own
body.

[Woodward] claims under three acts of the legislature of
New Hampshire, the most material of which was passed on
the 27th of June, 1816, and is entitled, "an act to amend the
charter, and enlarge and improve the corporation of Dartmouth College." Among other alterations in the charter,
this act increases the number of trustees to twenty-one,
gives the appointment of the additional members to the
executive of the State, and creates a board of overseers,
with power to inspect and control the most important acts
of the trustees. This board consists of twenty-five persons.
The president of the senate, the speaker of the house of
representatives of New Hampshire, and the governor and
lieutenant governor of Vermont, for the time being, are to
be members ex officio [as a result of holding their offices].
The board is to be completed by the governor and council
of New Hampshire, who are also empowered to fill all vacancies which may occur. . . .

The majority of the trustees of the college have refused to accept this amended charter, and have brought this suit for the corporate property, which is in possession of a person holding by virtue of the acts which have been stated.

It can require no argument to prove, that the circumstances of this case constitute a contract. An application is made to the crown for a charter to incorporate a religious and literary institution. In the application, it is stated that large contributions have been made for the object, which will be conferred on the corporation, as soon as it shall be created. The charter is granted, and on its faith the property is conveyed. Surely in this transaction every ingredient of a complete and legitimate contract is to be found.

The points for consideration are,

(1) Is this contract protected by the Constitution of the United States?

(2) Is it impaired by the acts under which [Woodward] holds?

On the first point it has been argued, that the word "contract," in its broadest sense, would comprehend the political relations between the government and its citizens, would extend to offices held within a State for State purposes, and to many of those laws concerning civil institutions, which must change with circumstances, and be modified by ordinary legislation, which deeply concern the public, and which, to preserve good government, the public judgment must control. That even marriage is a contract, and its obligations are affected by the laws respecting divorces. That the clause in the Constitution, if construed [interpreted] in its greatest latitude would prohibit these laws. Taken in its broad unlimited sense, the clause would be an unprofitable and vexatious interference with the internal concerns of a State, would unnecessarily and unwisely embarrass its legislation, and render immutable those civil institutions which are established for purposes of internal government, and which, to subserve those purposes, ought to vary with varying circumstances. That as the framers of the Constitution could never have intended to insert in that instrument a provision so unnecessary, so mischievous, and so repugnant to its general spirit, the term "contract" must be understood in a more limited sense. That it must be understood as intended to guard against a power of at least doubtful utility, the abuse of which had been extensively felt, and to restrain the legislature in future from violating the right to property. That anterior to the formation of the Constitution, a course of legislation had prevailed in many, if not in all, of the States, which weakened the confidence of man in man, and embarrassed all transactions between individuals, by dispensing with a faithful performance of engagements. To correct this mischief, by restraining the power which produced it, the State legislatures were forbidden "to pass any law impairing the obligation of contracts," that is, of contracts respecting property, under which some individual could claim a right to something beneficial to himself; and that since the clause in the Constitution must in construction receive some limitation, it may be confined, and ought to be confined, to cases of this description, to cases within the mischief it was intended to remedy.

The general correctness of these observations cannot be controverted. That the framers of the Constitution did not intend to restrain the States in the regulation of their civil institutions, adopted for internal government, and that the instrument they have given us, is not to be so construed, may be admitted. The provision of the Constitution never has been understood to embrace other contracts than those which respect property, or some object of value, and confer rights which may be asserted in a court of justice. It never has been understood to restrict the general right of the legislature to legislate on the subject of divorces. Those acts enable some tribunal, not to impair a marriage contract, but to liberate one of the parties because it has been broken by the other. When any State legislature shall pass an act annulling all marriage contracts, or allowing either party to annul it without the consent of the other, it will be time enough to inquire whether such an act be constitutional.

The parties in this case differ less on general principles, less on the true construction of the Constitution in the abstract, than on the application of those principles to this case, and on the true construction of the charter of 1769. This is the point on which the cause essentially depends. If the act of incorporation be a grant of political power, if it create a civil institution to be employed in the administration of the government, or if the funds of the college be public property, or if the State of New Hampshire, as a government, be alone interested in its transactions, the subject is one in which the legislature of the State may act according to its own judgment, unrestrained by any limitation of its power imposed by the Constitution of the United States.

But if this be a private eleemosynary [charitable] institution, endowed with a capacity to take property for objects unconnected with government, whose funds are bestowed by individuals on the faith of the charter - if the donors have stipulated for the future disposition and management of those funds in the manner prescribed by themselves - there may be more difficulty in the case, although neither the persons who have made these stipulations, nor those for whose benefit they were made, should be parties to the cause. Those who are no longer interested in the property may yet retain such an interest in the preservation of their own arrangements as to have a right to insist that those arrangements shall be held sacred. Or, if they have themselves disappeared, it becomes a subject of serious and anxious inquiry whether those whom they have legally empowered to represent them forever may not assert all the rights which they possessed while in being, whether, if they be without personal representatives who may feel injured by a violation of the compact, the trustees be not so completely their representatives in the eye of the law as to stand in their place, not only as respects the government of the college but also as respects the maintenance of the college charter.

It becomes then the duty of the Court most seriously to examine this charter, and to ascertain its true character.

From the instrument itself, it appears that about the year 1754, the Reverend Eleazer Wheelock established at his own expense, and on his own estate, a charity school for the instruction of Indians in the Christian religion. The success of this institution inspired him with the design of soliciting contributions in England for carrying on and extending his undertaking. In this pious work he employed the Reverend Nathaniel Whitaker, who, by virtue of a power of attorney from Dr. Wheelock, appointed the Earl of Dartmouth and others, trustees of the money, which had been, and should be, contributed, which appointment Dr. Wheelock confirmed by a deed of trust authorizing the trustees to fix on a site for the college. They determined to establish the school on Connecticut river, in the western part of New Hampshire, that situation being supposed favorable for carrying on the original design among the Indians, and also for promoting learning among the English, and the proprietors in the neighborhood having made large offers of land on condition that the college should there be placed. Dr. Wheelock then applied to the crown for an act of incorporation, and represented the expediency of appointing those whom he had, by his last will, named as trustees in America to be members of the proposed corporation. "In consideration of the premises," " for the education and instruction of the youth of the Indian tribes," etc. "and also of English youth, and any others," the charter was granted, and the trustees of Dartmouth College were by that name created a body corporate, with power, for the use of the said college, to acquire real and personal property, and to pay the president, tutors, and other officers of the college such salaries as they shall allow.

The charter proceeds to appoint Eleazer Wheelock, "the founder of said college," president thereof, with power by his last will to appoint a successor, who is to continue in office until disapproved by the trustees. In case of vacancy, the trustees may appoint a president, and in case of the ceasing of a president, the senior professor or tutor, being one of the trustees, shall exercise the office until an appointment shall be made. The trustees have power to appoint and displace professors, tutors, and other officers, and to supply any vacancies which may be created in their own body, by death, resignation, removal, or disability, and also to make orders, ordinances, and laws for the government of the college, the same not being repugnant to the laws of Great Britain or of New Hampshire, and not excluding any person on account of his speculative sentiments in religion, or his being of a religious profession different from that of the trustees.

This charter was accepted, and the property both real and personal, which had been contributed for the benefit of the college, was conveyed to, and vested in, the corporate body.

From this brief review of the most essential parts of the charter, it is apparent that the funds of the college consisted entirely of private donations. It is, perhaps, not very important who were the donors. The probability is that the Earl of Dartmouth and the other trustees in England were, in fact, the largest contributors. Yet the legal conclusion, from the facts recited in the charter, would probably be that Dr. Wheelock was the founder of the college.

The origin of the institution was, undoubtedly, the Indian charity school, established by Dr. Wheelock at his own expense. It was at his instance, and to enlarge this school, that contributions were solicited in England. The person soliciting these contributions was his agent, and the trustees, who received the money, were appointed by, and act under, his authority. It is not too much to say that the funds were obtained by him, in trust, to be applied by him to the purposes of his enlarged school. The charter of incorporation was granted at his instance. The persons named by him in his last will as the trustees of his charity school compose a part of the corporation, and he is declared to be the founder of the college and its president for life. Were the inquiry material, we should feel some hesitation in saying that Dr. Wheelock was not, in law, to be considered as the founder of this institution, and as possessing all the rights appertaining to that character. But be this as it may, Dartmouth College is really endowed by private individuals, who have bestowed their funds for the propagation of the Christian religion among the Indians, and for the promotion of piety and learning generally. From these funds the salaries of the tutors are drawn; and these salaries lessen the expense of education to the students. It is then [a charity] and, as far as respects its funds, a private corporation.

Do its objects stamp on it a different character? Are the trustees and professors public officers, invested with any portion of political power, partaking in any degree in the administration of civil government, and performing duties which flow from the sovereign authority?

That education is an object of national concern, and a proper subject of legislation, all admit. That there may be an institution founded by government, and placed entirely under its immediate control, the officers of which would be public officers, amenable exclusively to government, none will deny. But is Dartmouth College such an institution? Is education altogether in the hands of government? Does every teacher of youth become a public officer, and do donations for the purpose of education necessarily become public property, so far that the will of the legislature, not the will of the donor, becomes the law of the donation? These questions are of serious moment to society, and deserve to be well considered.

Doctor Wheelock, as the keeper of his charity school, instructing the Indians in the art of reading, and in our holy religion, sustaining them at his own expense, and on the voluntary contributions of the charitable, could scarcely be considered as a public officer, exercising any portion of those duties which belong to government; nor could the legislature have supposed that his private funds, or those given by others, were subject to legislative management, because they were applied to the purposes of education. When, afterwards, his school was enlarged, and the liberal contributions made in England, and in America, enabled him to extend his cares to the education of the youth of his own country, no change was wrought in his own character, or in the nature of his duties. Had he employed assistant tutors with the funds contributed by others, or had the trustees in England established a school with Dr. Wheelock at its head, and paid salaries to him and his assistants, they would still have been private tutors; and the fact that they were employed in the education of youth could not have converted them into public officers, concerned in the administration of public duties, or have given the legislature a right to interfere in the management of the fund. The trustees, in whose care that fund was placed by the contributors, would have been permitted to execute their trust uncontrolled by legislative authority.

Whence, then, can be derived the idea that Dartmouth College has become a public institution, and its trustees public officers, exercising powers conferred by the public for public objects? Not from the source whence its funds were drawn, for its foundation is purely private and [charitable]. Not from the application of those funds, for money may be given for education, and the persons receiving it do not, by being employed in the education of youth, become members of the civil government. Is it from the act of incorporation? Let this subject be considered.

A corporation is an artificial being, invisible, intangible, and existing only in contemplation of law. Being the mere creature of law, it possesses only those properties which the charter of its creation confers upon it, either expressly, or as incidental to its very existence. These are such as are supposed best calculated to effect the object for which it was created. Among the most important are immortality, and, if the expression may be allowed, individuality; properties by which a perpetual succession of many persons are considered as the same, and may act as a single individual. They enable a corporation to manage its own affairs, and to hold property without the perplexing intricacies, the hazardous and endless necessity of perpetual conveyances for the purpose of transmitting it from hand to hand. It is chiefly for the purpose of clothing bodies of men, in succession, with these qualities and capacities, that corporations were invented, and are in use. By these means, a perpetual succession of individuals are capable of acting for the promotion of the particular object, like one immortal being. But this being does not share in the civil government of the country, unless that be the purpose for which it was created. Its immortality no more confers on it political power, or a political character, than immortality would confer such power or character on a natural person. It is no more a State instrument than a natural person exercising the same powers would be. If, then, a natural person, employed by individuals in the education of youth, or for the government of a seminary in which youth is educated, would not become a public officer, or be considered as a member, of the civil government, how is it that this artificial being, created by law, for the purpose of being employed by the same individuals for the same purposes, should become a part of the civil government of the country? Is it because its existence, its capacities, its powers are given by law? Because the government has given it the power to take and to hold property in a particular form, and for particular purposes, has the government a consequent right substantially to change that form, or to vary the purposes to which the property is to be applied? This principle has never been asserted or recognized, and is supported by no authority. Can it derive aid from reason?

The objects for which a corporation is created are universally such as the government wishes to promote. They are deemed beneficial to the country; and this benefit constitutes the consideration, and, in most cases, the sole consideration of the grant. In most [charitable] institutions, the object would be difficult, perhaps unattainable, without the aid of a charter of incorporation. Charitable, or public spirited individuals, desirous of making permanent appropriations for charitable or other useful purposes, find it impossible to effect their design securely, and certainly, without an incorporating act. They apply to the government, state their beneficent object, and offer to advance the money necessary for its accomplishment, provided the government will confer on the instrument which is to execute their designs the capacity to execute them. The proposition is considered and approved. The benefit to the public is considered as an ample compensation for the faculty it confers, and the corporation is created. If the advantages to the public constitute a full compensation for the faculty it gives, there can be no reason for exacting a further compensation, by claiming a right to exercise over this artificial being a power which changes its nature, and touches the fund, for the security and application of which it was created. There can be no reason for implying in a charter, given for a valuable consideration, a power which is not only not expressed, but is in direct contradiction to its express stipulations.

From the fact, then, that a charter of incorporation has been granted, nothing can be inferred which changes the character of the institution, or transfers to the government any new power over it. The character of civil institutions does not grow out of their incorporation, but out of the manner in which they are formed, and the objects for which they are created. The right to change them is not founded on their being incorporated, but on their being the instruments of government, created for its purposes. The same institutions, created for the same objects, though not incorporated, would be public institutions, and, of course, be controllable by the legislature. The incorporating act neither gives nor prevents this control. Neither, in reason, can the incorporating act change the character of a private [charitable] institution.

We are next led to the inquiry, for whose benefit the property given to Dartmouth College was secured? [Woodward has] insisted, that the beneficial interest is in the people of New Hampshire. The charter, after reciting the preliminary measures which had been taken, and the application for an act of incorporation, proceeds thus:

"Know ye, therefore, that we, considering the premise; and being willing to encourage the laudable and charitable design of spreading Christian knowledge among the savages of our American wilderness, and, also, that the best means of education be established in our province of New-Hampshire for the benefit of said province, do, of our special grace," etc.

Do these expressions bestow on New Hampshire any exclusive right to the property of the college, any exclusive interest in the labors of the professors? Or do they merely indicate a willingness that New Hampshire should enjoy those advantages which result to all from the establishment of a seminary of learning in the neighborhood? On this point we think if impossible to entertain a serious doubt. The words themselves, unexplained by the context, indicate, that the "benefit intended for the province" is that which is derived from "establishing the best means of education therein," that is, from establishing in the province Dartmouth College, as constituted by the charter. But, if these words, considered alone, could admit of doubt, that doubt is completely removed by an inspection of the entire instrument.

The particular interests of New Hampshire never entered into the mind of the donors, never constituted a motive for their donation. The propagation of the Christian religion among the savages, and the dissemination of useful knowledge among the youth of the country, were the avowed and the sole objects of their contributions. In these, New Hampshire would participate; but nothing particular or exclusive was intended for her. Even the site of the college was selected, not for the sake of New Hampshire, but because it was "most subservient to the great ends in view," and because liberal donations of land were offered by the proprietors, on condition that the institution should be there established. The real advantages from the location of the college, are, perhaps, not less considerable to those on the west, than to those on the east side of Connecticut River. The clause which constitutes the incorporation, and expresses the objects for which it was made, declares those objects to be the instruction of the Indians, "and also of English youth, and any others." So that the objects of the contributors, and the incorporating act, were the same - the promotion of Christianity, and of education generally, not the interests of New Hampshire particularly.

From this review of the charter, it appears that Dartmouth College is [a charitable] institution, incorporated for the purpose of perpetuating the application of the bounty of the donors, to the specified objects of that bounty - that its trustees or governors were originally named by the founder, and invested with the power of perpetuating themselves, that they are not public officers, nor is it a civil institution, participating in the administration of government, but a charity school, or a seminary of education, incorporated for the preservation of its property, and the perpetual application of that property to the objects of its creation.

Yet a question remains to be considered, of more real difficulty, on which more doubt has been entertained than on all that have been discussed. The founders of the college, at least those whose contributions were in money, have parted with the property bestowed upon it, and their representatives have no interest in that property. The donors of land are equally without interest, so long as the corporation shall exist. Could they be found, they are unaffected by any alteration in its Constitution, and probably regardless of its form, or even of its existence. The students are fluctuating, and no individual among our youth has a vested interest in the institution, which can be asserted in a Court of justice. Neither the founders of the college, nor the youth for whose benefit it was founded, complain of the alteration made in its charter, or think themselves injured by it. The trustees alone complain, and the trustees have no beneficial interest to be protected. Can this be such a contract as the Constitution intended to withdraw from the power of State legislation? Contracts, the parties to which have a vested beneficial interest, and those only, it has been said, are the objects about which the Constitution is solicitous, and to which its protection is extended.

The Court has bestowed on this argument the most deliberate consideration, and the result will be stated. Dr. Wheelock, acting for himself, and for those who, at his solicitation, had made contributions to his school, applied for this charter, as the instrument which should enable him, and them, to perpetuate their beneficent intention. It was granted. An artificial, immortal being was created by the crown, capable of receiving and distributing forever, according to the will of the donors, the donations which should be made to it. On this being, the contributions which had been collected were immediately bestowed. These gifts were made, not indeed to make a profit for the donors or their posterity, but for something in their opinion of inestimable value, for something which they deemed a full equivalent for the money with which it was purchased. The consideration for which they stipulated [settled], is the perpetual application of the fund to its object, in the mode prescribed by themselves. Their descendants may take no interest in the preservation of this consideration. But in this respect their descendants are not their representatives. They are represented by the corporation. The corporation is the assignee of their rights, stands in their place, and distributes their bounty, as they would themselves have distributed it, had they been immortal. So with respect to the students who are to derive learning from this source. The corporation is a trustee for them also. Their potential rights, which, taken distributively, are imperceptible, amount collectively to a most important interest. These are, in the aggregate, to be exercised, asserted and protected by the corporation. . . .

According to the theory of the British Constitution, their parliament is omnipotent. To annul corporate rights might give a shock to public opinion, which that government has chosen to avoid; but its power is not questioned. Had parliament, immediately after the emanation of this charter, and the execution of those conveyances which followed it, annulled the instrument, so that the living donors would have witnessed the disappointment of their hopes, the perfidy of the transaction would have been universally acknowledged. Yet then, as now, the donors would have had no interest in the property; then, as now, those who might be students would have had no rights to be violated; then, as now, it might be said that the trustees, in whom the rights of all were combined, possessed no private, individual, beneficial interest in the property confided to their protection. Yet the contract would at that time have been deemed sacred by all. What has since occurred to strip it of its inviolability? Circumstances have not changed it. In reason, in justice, and in law, it is now what it was in 1769.

This is plainly a contract to which the donors, the trustees, and the crown (to whose rights and obligations New Hampshire succeeds), were the original parties. It is a contract made on a valuable consideration. It is a contract for the security and disposition of property. It is a contract, on the faith of which real and personal estate has been conveyed to the corporation. It is then a contract within the letter of the Constitution, and within its spirit also, unless the fact that the property is invested by the donors in trustees for the promotion of religion and education, for the benefit of persons who are perpetually changing, though the objects remain the same, shall create a particular exception, taking this case out of the prohibition contained in the Constitution.

It is more than possible that the preservation of rights of this description was not particularly in the view of the framers of the Constitution when the clause under consideration was introduced into that instrument. It is probable that interferences of more frequent recurrence, to which the temptation was stronger, and of which the mischief was more extensive, constituted the great motive for imposing this restriction on the State legislatures. But although

a particular and a rare case may not, in itself, be of sufficient magnitude to induce a rule, yet it must be governed by
the rule when established, unless some plain and strong reason for excluding it can be given. It is not enough to say
that this particular case was not in the mind of the convention when the article was framed, nor of the American
people when it was adopted. It is necessary to go farther,
and to say that had this particular case been suggested, the
language would have been so varied as to exclude it, or it
would have been made a special exception. . . .

There is no expression in the Constitution, no sentiment
delivered by its contemporaneous expounders, which would
justify us in making it. In the absence of all authority of
this kind, is there in the nature and reason of the case itself
that which would sustain a construction of the Constitution
not warranted by its words? Are contracts of this description of a character to excite so little interest that we must
exclude them from the provisions of the Constitution as
being unworthy of the attention of those who framed the
instrument? Or does public policy so imperiously demand
their remaining exposed to legislative alteration as to compel us, or rather permit us to say, that these words which
were introduced to give stability to contracts, and which in
their plain import comprehend this contract, must yet be so
construed as to exclude it?

Almost all [charitable] corporations, those which are created for the promotion of religion, of charity, or of education, are of the same character. The law of this case is the
law of all. In every literary or charitable institution, unless
the objects of the bounty be themselves incorporated, the
whole legal interest is in trustees, and can be asserted only
by them. The donors or claimants of the bounty, if they
can appear in Court at all, can appear only to complain of
the trustees. In all other situations, they are identified with,
and personated by, the trustees; and their rights are to be

defended and maintained by them. Religion, charity, and education are in the law of England legatees or donees, capable of receiving bequest or donations in this form. They appear in Court, and claim or defend by the corporation. Are they of so little estimation in the United States that contracts for their benefit must be excluded from the protection of words, which in their natural import include them? Or do such contracts so necessarily require new modeling by the authority of the legislature, that the ordinary rules of construction must be disregarded in order to leave them exposed to legislative alteration?

All feel that these objects are not deemed unimportant in the United States. The interest which this case has excited proves that they are not. The framers of the Constitution did not deem them unworthy of its care and protection. They have, though in a different mode, manifested their respect for science, by reserving to the government of the union the power "to promote the progress of science and useful arts, by securing for limited times, to authors and inventors, the exclusive right to their respective writings and discoveries." They have so far withdrawn science and the useful arts from the action of the State governments. Why then should they be supposed so regardless of contracts made for the advancement of literature as to intend to exclude them from provisions made for the security of ordinary contracts between man and man? No reason for making this supposition is perceived.

If the insignificance of the object does not require that we should exclude contracts respecting it from the protection of the Constitution; neither, as we conceive, is the policy of leaving them subject to legislative alteration so apparent as to require a forced construction of that instrument in order to effect it. These [charitable] institutions do not fill the place which would otherwise be occupied by government, but that which would otherwise remain vacant. They are complete acquisitions to literature. They are donations to education, donations which any government must be disposed rather to encourage than to discountenance. It requires no very critical examination of the human mind to enable us to determine that one great inducement to these gifts is the conviction felt by the giver that the disposition he makes of them is immutable. It is probable that no man ever was, and that no man ever will be, the founder of a college, believing at the time that an act of incorporation constitutes no security for the institution, believing that it is immediately to be deemed a public institution, whose funds are to be governed and applied not by the will of the donor but by the will of the legislature. All such gifts are made in the pleasing, perhaps delusive hope, that the charity will flow forever in the channel which the givers have marked out for it. If every man finds in his own bosom strong evidence of the universality of this sentiment, there can be but little reason to imagine that the framers of our Constitution were strangers to it, and that, feeling the necessity and policy of giving permanence and security to contracts, of withdrawing them from the influence of legislative bodies, whose fluctuating policy and repeated interferences produced the most perplexing and injurious embarrassments, they still deemed it necessary to leave these contracts subject to those interferences. The motives for such an exception must be very powerful, to justify the construction which makes it.

The motives suggested . . . grow out of the original appointment of the trustees, which is supposed to have been in a spirit hostile to the genius of our government, and the presumption that, if allowed to continue themselves, they now are, and must remain forever, what they originally were. Hence is inferred the necessity of applying to this corporation, and to other similar corporations, the correcting and improving hand of the legislature.

It has been urged repeatedly, and certainly with a degree of earnestness which attracted attention, that the trustees deriving their power from a regal source must necessarily partake of the spirit of their origin, and that their first principles, unimproved by that resplendent light which has been shed around them, must continue to govern the college, and to guide the students. Before we inquire into the influence which this argument ought to have on the Constitutional question, it may not be amiss to examine the fact on which it rests. . . . The original trustees . . . were named by Dr. Wheelock, and those who were added to his nomination, most probably with his approbation, were among the most eminent and respectable individuals in New Hampshire.

The only evidence which we possess of the character of Dr. Wheelock is furnished by this charter. The judicious means employed for the accomplishment of his object, and the success which attended his endeavors, would lead to the opinion that he united a sound understanding to that humanity and benevolence which suggested his undertaking. It surely cannot he assumed that his trustees were selected without judgment. With as little probability can it be assumed, that, while the light of science and of liberal principles pervades the whole community, these originally benighted trustees remain in utter darkness, incapable of participating in the general improvement - that, while the human race is rapidly advancing, they are stationary. Reasoning a priori [by deduction], we should believe that learned and intelligent men, selected by its patrons for the government of a literary institution, would select learned and intelligent men for their successors, men as well fitted for the government of a college as those who might be chosen by other means. Should this reasoning ever prove erroneous in a particular case, public opinion . . . would correct the institution. The mere possibility of the contrary would not justify a construction of the Constitution which should exclude these contracts from the protection of a provision whose terms comprehend them.

The opinion of the Court, after mature deliberation, is, that this is a contract, the obligation of which cannot be impaired without violating the Constitution of the United States. This opinion appears to us to be equally supported by reason, and by the former decisions of this Court.

We next proceed to the inquiry whether its obligation has been impaired by those acts of the legislature of New Hampshire, to which the special verdict refers.

From the review of this charter, which has been taken, it appears, that the whole power of governing the college, of appointing and removing tutors, of fixing their salaries, of directing the course of study to be pursued by the students, and of filling up vacancies created in their own body, was vested in the trustees. On the part of the crown it was expressly stipulated: that this corporation, thus constituted, should continue forever; and that the number of trustees should forever consist of twelve, and no more. By this contract the crown was bound, and could have made no violent alteration in its essential terms without impairing its obligation.

By the revolution, the duties, as well as the powers, of government devolved on the people of New Hampshire. It is admitted that among the latter was comprehended the transcendent power of Parliament, as well as that of the executive department. It is too clear to require the support of argument, that all contracts and rights respecting property remained unchanged by the revolution. The obligations then, which were created by the charter to Dartmouth College, were the same in the new that they had been in the old government. The power of the government was also the same. A repeal of this charter at any time prior to the adoption of the present Constitution of the United States would have been an extraordinary and unprecedented act of power, but one which could have been contested only by the restrictions upon the legislature to be found in the Constitution of the State. But the Constitution of the United States has imposed this additional limitation - that the legislature of a State shall pass no act "impairing the obligation of contracts."

It has been already stated that the act "to amend the charter, and enlarge and improve the corporation of Dartmouth College" increases the number of trustees to twenty-one, gives the appointment of the additional members to the executive of the State, and creates a board of overseers, to consist of twenty-five persons, of whom twenty-one are also appointed by the executive of New Hampshire, who have power to inspect and control the most important acts of the trustees.

On the effect of this law, two opinions cannot be entertained. Between acting directly, and acting through the agency of trustees and overseers, no essential difference is perceived. The whole power of governing the college is transferred from trustees appointed according to the will of the founder, expressed in the charter, to the executive of New Hampshire. The management and application of the funds of this [charitable] institution, which are placed by the donors in the hands of trustees named in the charter, and empowered to perpetuate themselves, are placed by this act under the control of the government of the State. The will of the State is substituted for the will of the donors, in every essential operation of the college. This is not an immaterial change. The founders of the college contracted, not merely for the perpetual application of the funds which they gave, to the objects for which those funds were given; they contracted also to secure that application by the constitution of the corporation. They contracted for a system which should, as far as human foresight can provide, retain forever the government of the literary institution they had formed, in the hands of persons approved by themselves. This system is totally changed. The charter of 1769 exists no longer. It is reorganized, and reorganized in such a manner, as to convert a literary institution, molded according to the will of its founders, and placed under the control of private literary men, into a machine entirely subservient to the will of government. This may be for the advantage of this college in particular, and may be for the advantage of literature in general; but it is not according to the will of the donors, and is subversive of that contract on the faith of which their property was given.

In the view which has been taken of this interesting case, the Court has confined itself to the rights possessed by the trustees, as the assignees and representatives of the donors and founders, for the benefit of religion and literature. . . .

[T]he Court [is of the opinion], on general principles, that in these private [charitable] institutions, the body corporate, as possessing the whole legal and equitable interest, and completely representing the donors for the purpose of executing the trust, has rights which are protected by the Constitution.

It results from this opinion that the acts of the legislature of New Hampshire, which are stated in the special verdict found in this cause, are repugnant to the Constitution of the United States, and that the judgment on this special verdict ought to have been for [Dartmouth]. The judgment of the State Court must, therefore, be reversed.

Women's Work
Louis Brandeis Fights For Working Women's Rights
Muller v. Oregon

Man's work lasts till set of sun;
Woman's work is never done.
- Unknown (c.1655)

In reaction to the unchecked excesses of industrialization, many states enacted protective wage and hour labor laws. In 1902 the U.S. Supreme Court struck down New York's ten-hour day for male workers, calling the law a "meddlesome interference."

On February 19, 1903 the Oregon legislature enacted a ten-hour day for women workers. Oregon joined seventeen other states which had previously enacted similar limitations on the hours women could work: Massachusetts (1874), North and South Dakota (1877), Rhode Island (1885), Louisiana (1886), Connecticut, Maine, and New Hampshire (1887), Maryland (1888), Virginia and Oklahoma (1890), New Jersey (1892), Pennsylvania and Wisconsin (1897), Nebraska and New York (1899), and Washington (1901). The reasons for enacting this kind of protective legislation for women were variously given as "the physical organization of women, the maternal functions of women, the rearing and education of children, the maintenance of the home."

On September 4, 1905 Mrs. Emma Gotcher, a woman employed at the Grand Laundry in Portland, Oregon, was ordered by her supervisor to work more than ten hours. Gotcher's employer, Curt Muller, was tried and convicted in a Multnomah County Court of violating Oregon's Ten-Hour Day for Women Workers Law. The Oregon Supreme Court upheld his conviction. Muller appealed to the U.S. Supreme Court. Oregon hired Boston lawyer Louis D. Brandeis to represent them. Brandeis revolutionized Supreme Court practice by filing a brief with the Court filled not with past legal precedents but with current economic and sociological facts.

On February 24, 1908 the 9-0 decision of the United States Supreme Court was announced by Justice David Brewer.

The *Women's Work* Court

Chief Justice Melville Fuller
Appointed Chief Justice by President Cleveland
Served 1888 - 1910

Associate Justice John Marshall Harlan
Appointed by President Hayes
Served 1877 - 1911

Associate Justice David Brewer
Appointed by President Benjamin Harrison
Served 1889 - 1910

Associate Justice Edward White
Appointed by President Cleveland
Served 1894 - 1921

Associate Justice Rufus Peckham
Appointed by President Cleveland
Served 1895 - 1909

Associate Justice Joseph McKenna
Appointed by President McKinley
Served 1898 - 1925

Associate Justice Oliver Wendell Holmes, Jr.
Appointed by President Theodore Roosevelt
Served 1902 - 1932

Associate Justice William Day
Appointed by President Theodore Roosevelt
Served 1903 - 1922

Associate Justice William Moody
Appointed by President Theodore Roosevelt
Served 1906 - 1910

The unedited legal text of *Muller v. Oregon* can be found in volume 208 of *United States Reports* beginning on page 412. Our edited plain-English text follows.

Muller v. Oregon
February 24, 1908

Justice David Brewer: On February 19, 1903, the legislature of the State of Oregon passed an act the first section of which is in these words:

Section 1. That no female [shall] be employed in any mechanical establishment, or factory, or laundry in this State more than ten hours during any one day. The hours of work may be so arranged as to permit the employment of females at any time so that they shall not work more than ten hours during the twenty-four hours of any one day.

. . . . On September 18, 1905, an information [accusation] was filed in the Circuit Court of the State for the County of Multnomah, charging that the defendant [Curt Muller] on the 4th day of September, 1905, in the county of Multnomah and State of Oregon, then and there being the owner of a laundry, known as the Grand Laundry, in the city of Portland, and the employer of females therein, did then and there unlawfully permit and suffer one Joe Haselbock, he, the said Joe Haselbock, then and there being an overseer, superintendent, and agent of said Curt Muller, in the said Grand Laundry, to require a female, to-wit, one Mrs. E. Gotcher, to work more than ten hours in said laundry on said 4th day of September, 1905, contrary to the statutes in such cases made and provided, and against the peace and dignity of the State of Oregon.

A trial resulted in a verdict against [Muller], who was sentenced to pay a fine of $10. The Supreme Court of the State affirmed [let stand] the conviction, whereupon the case was brought here. . . .

The single question is the constitutionality of the statute under which [Muller] was convicted so far as it affects the work of a female in a laundry. That it does not conflict with any provisions of the State Constitution is settled by the decision of the Supreme Court of the State. The contentions of [Muller] are thus stated . . . :

1. Because the statute attempts to prevent persons . . . from making their own contracts, and thus violates the provisions of the Fourteenth Amendment, as follows:

   No State shall make or enforce any law which shall abridge the privileges or immunities of citizens of the United States; nor shall any State deprive any person of life, liberty, or property, without due process of law; nor deny to any person within its jurisdiction the equal protection of the laws.

2. Because the statute does not apply equally to all persons similarly situated. . . .

3. The statute is not a valid exercise of the police power. The kinds of work prescribed are not unlawful, nor are they declared to be immoral or dangerous to the public health; nor can such a law be sustained [approved] on the ground that it is designed to protect women on account of their sex. There is no necessary or reasonable connection between the limitation prescribed by the act and the public health, safety, or welfare.

It is the law of Oregon that women, whether married or single, have equal contractual and personal rights with men. As said by [Oregon's] Chief Justice Wolverton . . . , after a review of the various statutes of the State upon the subject:

We may therefore say with perfect confidence that, with these three sections upon the statute book, the wife can deal not only with her separate property, acquired from whatever source, in the same manner as her husband can with property belonging to him, but that she may make contracts and incur liabilities, and the same may be enforced against her, the same as if she were a femme sole. There is now no residuum of civil disability resting upon her which is not recognized as existing against the husband. The current runs steadily and strongly in the direction of the emancipation of the wife, and the policy, as disclosed by all recent legislation upon the subject in this State, is to place her upon the same footing as if she were a femme sole not only with respect to her separate property, but as it affects her right to make binding contracts; and the most natural corollary to the situation is that the remedies for the enforcement of liabilities incurred are made coextensive and coequal with such enlarged conditions.

It thus appears that, putting to one side the elective franchise, in the matter of personal and contractual rights, they stand on the same plane as the other sex. Their rights in these respects can no more be infringed than the equal rights of their brothers. We [the United States Supreme Court] held in *Lochner v. New York* that a law providing that no laborer shall be required or permitted to work in bakeries more than sixty hours in a week or ten hours in a day was not, as to men, a legitimate exercise of the police power of the State, but an unreasonable, unnecessary, and arbitrary interference with the right and liberty of the individual to contract in relation to his labor, and, as such, was in conflict with, and void under, the Federal Constitution. That decision is invoked by [Muller] as decisive of the question before us. But this assumes that the difference between the sexes does not justify a different rule respecting a restriction of the hours of labor.

In patent cases, counsel are apt to open the argument with a discussion of the state of the art. It may not be amiss, in the present case, before examining the constitutional question, to notice the course of legislation, as well as expressions of opinion from other than judicial sources. In the brief filed by Louis D. Brandeis for the [State of Oregon] is a very copious collection of all these matters. . . .

The legislation and opinions referred to . . . may not be, technically speaking, authorities, and in them is little or no discussion of the constitutional question presented to us for determination, yet they are significant of a widespread belief that woman's physical structure, and the functions she performs in consequence thereof, justify special legislation restricting or qualifying the conditions under which she should be permitted to toil. Constitutional questions, it is true, are not settled by even a consensus of present public opinion, for it is the peculiar value of a written constitution that it places in unchanging form limitations upon legislative action, and thus gives a permanence and stability to popular government which otherwise would be lacking. At the same time, when a question of fact is debated and debatable, and the extent to which a special constitutional limitation goes is affected by the truth in respect to that fact, a widespread and long-continued belief concerning it is worthy of consideration. We take judicial cognizance of all matters of general knowledge.

It is undoubtedly true, as more than once declared by this Court, that the general right to contract in relation to one's business is part of the liberty of the individual, protected by the Fourteenth Amendment to the Federal Constitution; yet it is equally well settled that this liberty is not absolute and extending to all contracts, and that a State may, without conflicting with the provisions of the Fourteenth Amendment, restrict in many respects the individual's power of contract. . . .

That woman's physical structure and the performance of maternal functions place her at a disadvantage in the struggle for subsistence is obvious. This is especially true when the burdens of motherhood are upon her. Even when they are not, by abundant testimony of the medical fraternity, continuance for a long time on her feet at work, repeating this from day to day, tends to injurious effects upon the body, and, as healthy mothers are essential to vigorous offspring, the physical well-being of woman becomes an object of public interest and care in order to preserve the strength and vigor of the race.

Still again, history discloses the fact that woman has always been dependent upon man. He established his control at the outset by superior physical strength, and this control in various forms, with diminishing intensity, has continued to the present. As minors, though not to the same extent, she has been looked upon in the courts as needing especial care that her rights may be preserved. Education was long denied her, and while now the doors of the schoolroom are opened and her opportunities for acquiring knowledge are great, yet, even with that and the consequent increase of capacity for business affairs, it is still true that, in the struggle for subsistence, she is not an equal competitor with her brother. Though limitations upon personal and contractual rights may be removed by legislation, there is that in her disposition and habits of life which will operate against a full assertion of those rights. She will still be where some legislation to protect her seems necessary to secure a real equality of right. Doubtless there are individual exceptions, and there are many respects in which she has an advantage over him; but, looking at it from the viewpoint of the effort to maintain an independent position in life, she is not upon an equality. Differentiated by these matters from the other sex, she is properly placed in a class by herself, and legislation designed for her protection may be sustained even when like legislation is not necessary for men, and could not be sustained. It is impossible to close one's eyes to the fact that she still looks to her brother, and depends upon him. Even though all restrictions on political, personal, and contractual rights were taken away, and she stood, so far as statutes are concerned, upon an absolutely equal plane with him, it would still be true that she is so constituted that she will rest upon and look to him for protection; that her physical structure and a proper discharge of her maternal functions - having in view not merely her own health, but the well-being of the race - justify legislation to protect her from the greed, as well as the passion, of man. The limitations which this statute places upon her contractual powers, upon her right to agree with her employer as to the time she shall labor, are not imposed solely for her benefit, but also largely for the benefit of all. Many words cannot make this plainer. The two sexes differ in structure of body, in the functions to be performed by each, in the amount of physical strength, in the capacity for long-continued labor, particularly when done standing, the influence of vigorous health upon the future well-being of the race, the self-reliance which enables one to assert full rights, and in the capacity to maintain the struggle for subsistence. This difference justifies a difference in legislation, and upholds that which is designed to compensate for some of the burdens which rest upon her.

We have not referred in this discussion to the denial of the elective franchise in the State of Oregon, for, while that may disclose a lack of political equality in all things with her brother, that is not of itself decisive. The reason runs deeper, and rests in the inherent difference between the two sexes and in the different functions in life which they perform.

For these reasons, and without questioning in any respect the decision in *Lochner*, we are of the opinion that it cannot be adjudged that the act in question is in conflict with the

Federal Constitution so far as it respects the work of a female in a laundry, and the judgment of the Supreme Court of Oregon is affirmed.

The "Sick Chicken" Case
The Supreme Court Strikes Down FDR's New Deal
Schechter Poultry v. United States

It's more than a New Deal. It's a new world.
- F.D.R.'s Interior Secretary Harold Ickes

The New Deal was President Franklin D. Roosevelt's emergency legislative program to lift the nation out of the Great Depression. The centerpiece of The New Deal was the National Industrial Recovery Act. Signing the NIRA into law on June 16, 1933, President Roosevelt called it "the most important and far-reaching legislation ever enacted by the American Congress."

The National Industrial Recovery Act created a new federal agency, the National Recovery Administration (NRA), with the power to enact "codes" in order to regulate all *interstate commerce.* From 1933 through 1935 over seven hundred of these "codes" were enacted. On April 13, 1934 the National Recovery Administration enacted the "Live Poultry Code," giving the NRA regulatory power over the kosher chicken trade in New York City.

Four brothers, Aaron, Alex, Joseph, and Martin Schechter, owners of Schechter Poultry, a kosher chicken business operating in Brooklyn, New York, fell afoul of the NRA's "Live Poultry Code." They were indicted, tried, and convicted in U.S. District Court for multiple violations of the "Code," including a charge that they had sold a "sick chicken." On April 1, 1935 the U.S. Court of Appeals upheld their convictions.

The Schechters appealed to the U.S. Supreme Court. They argued that the New Deals' National Industrial Recovery Act was unconstitutional on two counts - first as an illegal delegation by Congress of their legislative power, a violation of the Constitution's Article I; and second as an illegal attempt by Congress to regulate *intrastate* commerce, a violation of the Constitution's Commerce Clause.

On May 27, 1935 the 9-0 decision of the U.S. Supreme Court was announced by Chief Justice Charles Evans Hughes.

The *"Sick Chicken"* Court

Chief Justice Charles Evans Hughes
Appointed Chief Justice by President Hoover
Served 1930 - 1941

Associate Justice Willis Van Devanter
Appointed by President Taft
Served 1910 - 1937

Associate Justice James McReynolds
Appointed by President Wilson
Served 1914 - 1941

Associate Justice Louis Brandeis
Appointed by President Wilson
Served 1916 - 1939

Associate Justice George Sutherland
Appointed by President Harding
Served 1922 - 1938

Associate Justice Pierce Butler
Appointed by President Harding
Served 1922 - 1939

Associate Justice Harlan Fiske Stone
Appointed by President Coolidge
Served 1925 - 1946

Associate Justice Owen Roberts
Appointed by President Hoover
Served 1930 - 1945

Associate Justice Benjamin Cardozo
Appointed by President Hoover
Served 1932 - 1938

The unedited legal text of *Schechter Poultry v. United States* can be found in volume 295 of *United States Reports* beginning on page 495. Our edited plain-English text follows.

Schechter Poultry v. United States
May 27, 1935

Chief Justice Charles Evans Hughes: [The owners of Schechter Poultry in Brooklyn, New York] were convicted in [United States District Court] of violations of . . . what is known as the "Live Poultry Code." . . . [Schechter Poultry] contended:

(1) that the Code had been adopted pursuant to an unconstitutional delegation by Congress of legislative power; and
(2) that it attempted to regulate intrastate transactions which lay outside the authority of Congress. . . .

The "Live Poultry Code" was approved by [President Franklin D. Roosevelt] on April 13, 1934. . . . The declared purpose is "to effect the policies of Title I of the National Industrial Recovery Act." . . . The President approved the Code by an Executive Order in which he found that the application for his approval had been duly made in accordance with the provisions of Title I of the National Industrial Recovery Act. . . .

Of the eighteen counts of the indictment [charge] . . . , two counts charged violation of the minimum wage and maximum hour provisions of the Code. . . . The charges in the ten counts, respectively, were that [Schechter Poultry], in selling to retail dealers and butchers, had permitted "selections of individual chickens taken from particular coops and half-coops."

Of the other six counts, one charged the sale to a butcher of an unfit chicken; two counts charged the making of sales without having the poultry inspected or approved in accordance with regulations or ordinances of the City of New York; two counts charged the making of false reports or the failure to make report relating to the range of daily prices and volume of sales for certain periods, and the remaining count was for sales to slaughterers or dealers who were without licenses required by the ordinances and regulations of the City of New York.

First. Two preliminary points are stressed by the Government with respect to the appropriate approach to the important questions presented. We are told that the provision of the statute authorizing the adoption of codes must be viewed in the light of the grave national crisis with which Congress was confronted. Undoubtedly, the conditions to which power is addressed are always to be considered when the exercise of power is challenged. Extraordinary conditions may call for extraordinary remedies. But the argument necessarily stops short of an attempt to justify action which lies outside the sphere of constitutional authority. Extraordinary conditions do not create or enlarge constitutional power. The Constitution established a national government with powers deemed to be adequate, as they have proved to be both in war and peace, but these powers of the national government are limited by the constitutional grants. Those who act under these grants are not at liberty to transcend the imposed limits because they believe that more or different power is necessary. Such assertions of extra-constitutional authority were anticipated and precluded by the explicit terms of the Tenth Amendment:

"The powers not delegated to the United States by the Constitution, nor prohibited by it to the States, are reserved to the States respectively, or to the people. . . ."

Second. The question of the delegation of legislative power. We recently had occasion to review the pertinent decisions and the general principles which govern the determination of this question. The Constitution provides that:

"All legislative powers herein granted shall be vested in a Congress of the United States, which shall consist of a Senate and House of Representatives."

Article I, Section 1. And the Congress is authorized "To make all laws which shall be necessary and proper for carrying into execution" its general powers.

Article I, Section 8, Paragraph 18. The Congress is not permitted to abdicate or to transfer to others the essential legislative functions with which it is thus vested.

We have repeatedly recognized the necessity of adapting legislation to complex conditions involving a host of details with which the national legislature cannot deal directly. . . . [T]he Constitution has never been regarded as denying to Congress the necessary resources of flexibility and practicality which will enable it to perform its function in laying down policies and establishing standards while leaving to selected instrumentalities the making of subordinate rules within prescribed limits, and the determination of facts to which the policy, as declared by the legislature, is to apply. But we said that the constant recognition of the necessity and validity of such provisions, and the wide range of administrative authority which has been developed by means of them, cannot be allowed to obscure the limitations of the authority to delegate, if our constitutional system is to be maintained.

. . . . Accordingly, we turn to the Recovery Act to ascertain what limits have been set to the exercise of the President's discretion. First, the President, as a condition of approval, is required to find that the trade or industrial associations or groups which propose a code, "impose no inequitable restrictions on admission to membership," and are "truly representative." That condition, however, relates only to the status of the initiators of the new laws, and not to the permissible scope of such laws. Second, the President is required to find that the code is not "designed to promote monopolies or to eliminate or oppress small enterprises, and will not operate to discriminate against them." And to this is added a proviso that the code "shall not permit monopolies or monopolistic practices." But these restrictions leave virtually untouched the field of policy envisaged by Section 1, and, in that wide field of legislative possibilities, the proponents of a code, refraining from monopolistic designs, may roam at will, and the President may approve or disapprove their proposals as he may see fit. That is the precise effect of the further finding that the President is to make - that the code "will tend to effectuate the policy of this title." While this is called a finding, it is really but a statement of an opinion as to the general effect upon the promotion of trade or industry of a scheme of laws. These are the only findings which Congress has made essential in order to put into operation a legislative code having the aims described in the "Declaration of Policy."

Nor is the breadth of the President's discretion left to the necessary implication of this limited requirement as to his findings. As already noted, the President, in approving a code, may impose his own conditions, adding to or taking from what is proposed as, "in his discretion," he thinks necessary "to effectuate the policy" declared by the Act. Of course, he has no less liberty when he prescribes a code on his own motion or on complaint, and he is free to prescribe one if a code has not been approved. The Act provides for the creation by the President of administrative agencies to assist him, but the action or reports of such agencies, or of his other assistants - their recommendations and findings in relation to the making of codes - have no sanction beyond the will of the President, who may accept, modify, or reject them as he pleases. Such recommendations or findings in no way limit the authority which Section 3 undertakes to vest in the President with no other conditions than those there specified. And this authority relates to a host of different trades and industries, thus extending the President's discretion to all the varieties of laws which he may deem to be beneficial in dealing with the vast array of commercial and industrial activities throughout the country.

Such a sweeping delegation of legislative power finds no support in the decisions upon which the Government especially relies. By the Interstate Commerce Act, Congress has itself provided a code of laws regulating the activities of the common carriers subject to the Act in order to assure the performance of their services upon just and reasonable terms, with adequate facilities and without unjust discrimination. Congress, from time to time, has elaborated its requirements as needs have been disclosed. To facilitate the application of the standards prescribed by the Act, Congress has provided an expert body. That administrative agency, in dealing with particular cases, is required to act upon notice and hearing, and its orders must be supported by findings of fact which, in turn, are sustained [upheld] by evidence. When the Commission is authorized to issue, for the construction, extension or abandonment of lines, a certificate of "public convenience and necessity," or to permit the acquisition by one carrier of the control of another, if that is found to be "in the public interest," we have pointed out that these provisions are not left without standards to guide determination. The authority conferred has direct relation to the standards prescribed for the service of common carriers, and can be exercised only upon findings, based upon evidence, with respect to particular conditions of transportation.

. . . . To summarize and conclude upon this point: Section 3 of the Recovery Act is without precedent. It supplies no standards for any trade, industry or activity. It does not undertake to prescribe rules of conduct to be applied to particular states of fact determined by appropriate administrative procedure. Instead of prescribing rules of conduct, it authorizes the making of codes to prescribe them. For that legislative undertaking, Section 3 sets up no standards, aside from the statement of the general aims of rehabilitation, correction and expansion described in Section 1. In view of the scope of that broad declaration, and of the nature of the few restrictions that are imposed, the discretion of the President in approving or prescribing codes, and thus enacting laws for the government of trade and industry throughout the country, is virtually unfettered. We think that the code-making authority this conferred is an unconstitutional delegation of legislative power.

Third. The question of the application of the provisions of the Live Poultry Code to intrastate transactions. Although the validity of the codes (apart from the question of delegation) rests upon the Commerce Clause of the Constitution, Section 3(a) is not, in terms, limited to interstate and foreign commerce. From the generality of its terms, and from the argument of the Government at the bar, it would appear that Section 3(a) was designed to authorize codes without that limitation. But, under Section 3(f), penalties are confined to violations of a code provision "in any transaction in or affecting interstate or foreign commerce." This aspect of the case presents the question whether the particular provisions of the Live Poultry Code, which the defendants [parties charged with an act] were convicted for violating and for having conspired to violate, were within the regulating power of Congress.

These provisions relate to the hours and wages of those employed by [Schechter Poultry] in their slaughterhouses in Brooklyn, and to the sales there made to retail dealers and butchers.

(1) Were these transactions "in" interstate commerce? Much is made of the fact that almost all the poultry coming to New York is sent there from other States. But the code provisions, as here applied, do not concern the transportation of the poultry from other States to New York, or the transactions of the commission men or others to whom it is consigned, or the sales made by such consignees to [Schechter Poultry]. When [Schechter Poultry] had made their purchases, whether at the West Washington Market in New York City or at the railroad terminals serving the City, or elsewhere, the poultry was trucked to their slaughterhouses in Brooklyn for local disposition. The interstate transactions in relation to that poultry then ended. [Schechter Poultry] held the poultry at their slaughterhouse markets for slaughter and local sale to retail dealers and butchers who, in turn, sold directly to consumers. Neither the slaughtering nor the sales by [Schechter Poultry] were transactions in interstate commerce.

The undisputed facts thus afford no warrant for the argument that the poultry handled by [Schechter Poultry] at their slaughterhouse markets was in a "current" or "flow" of interstate commerce, and was thus subject to congressional regulation. The mere fact that there may be a constant flow of commodities into a State does not mean that the flow continues after the property has arrived, and has become commingled with the mass of property within the State, and is there held solely for local disposition and use. So far as the poultry here in question is concerned, the flow in interstate commerce had ceased. The poultry had come to a permanent rest within the State. It was not held, used, or sold by [Schechter Poultry] in relation to any further transactions in interstate commerce, and was not destined for transportation to other States. Hence, decisions which deal with a stream of interstate commerce - where goods come to rest within a State temporarily and are later to go forward in interstate commerce - and with the regulations of transactions involved in that practical continuity of movement, are not applicable here.

(2) Did [Schechter Poultry's] transactions directly "affect" interstate commerce, so as to be subject to federal regulation? The power of Congress extends not only to the regulation of transactions which are part of interstate commerce, but to the protection of that commerce from injury. It matters not that the injury may be due to the conduct of those engaged in intrastate operations. Thus, Congress may protect the safety of those employed in interstate transportation "no matter what may be the source of the dangers which threaten it." . . . We [have previously ruled] that it is the "effect upon interstate commerce," not "the source of the injury," which is "the criterion of congressional power." We have held that, in dealing with common carriers engaged in both interstate and intrastate commerce, the dominant authority of Congress necessarily embraces the right to control their intrastate operations in all matters having such a close and substantial relation to interstate traffic that the control is essential or appropriate to secure the freedom of that traffic from interference or unjust discrimination and to promote the efficiency of the interstate service. And combinations and conspiracies to restrain interstate commerce, or to monopolize any part of it, are nonetheless within the reach of the Anti-Trust Act because the conspirators seek to attain their end by means of intrastate activities.

. . . . This is not a prosecution for a conspiracy to restrain or monopolize interstate commerce in violation of the Anti-Trust Act. [Schechter Poultry has] been convicted not upon direct charges of injury to interstate commerce or of interference with persons engaged in that commerce, but of violations of certain provisions of the Live Poultry Code and of conspiracy to commit these violations. Interstate commerce is brought in only upon the charge that violations of these provisions - as to hours and wages of employees and local sales - "affected" interstate commerce.

. . . . The question of chief importance relates to the provisions of the Code as to the hours and wages of those employed in [Schechter Poultry's] slaughterhouse markets. It is plain that these requirements are imposed in order to govern the details of [Schechter Poultry's] management of their local business. The persons employed in slaughtering and selling in local trade are not employed in interstate commerce. Their hours and wages have no direct relation to interstate commerce. The question of how many hours these employees should work and what they should be paid differs in no essential respect from similar questions in other local businesses which handle commodities brought into a State and there dealt in as a part of its internal commerce. This appears from an examination of the considerations urged by the Government with respect to conditions in the poultry trade. Thus, the Government argues that hours and wages affect prices; that slaughterhouse men sell at a small margin above operating costs, that labor represents fifty to sixty percent of these costs, that a slaughterhouse operator paying lower wages or reducing his cost by exacting long hours of work translates his saving into lower prices, that this results in demands for a cheaper grade of goods, and that the cutting of prices brings about a demoralization of the price structure. Similar conditions may be adduced in relation to other businesses. The argument of the Government proves too much. If the federal government may determine the wages and hours of employees in the internal commerce of a State, because of their relation to cost and prices and their indirect effect upon interstate commerce, it would seem that a similar control might be exerted over other elements of cost also affecting prices, such as the number of employees, rents, advertising, methods of doing business, etc. All the processes of production and distribution that enter into cost could likewise be controlled. If the cost of doing an intrastate business is, in itself, the permitted object of federal control, the extent of the regulation of cost would be a question of discretion, and not of power.

The Government also makes the point that efforts to enact state legislation establishing high labor standards have been impeded by the belief that, unless similar action is taken generally, commerce will be diverted from the States adopting such standards, and that this fear of diversion has led to demands for federal legislation on the subject of wages and hours. The apparent implication is that the federal authority under the commerce clause should be deemed to extend to the establishment of rules to govern wages and hours in intrastate trade and industry generally throughout the country, thus overriding the authority of the States to deal with domestic problems arising from labor conditions in their internal commerce.

It is not the province of the Court to consider the economic advantages or disadvantages of such a centralized system. It is sufficient to say that the Federal Constitution does not provide for it. Our growth and development have called for wide use of the commerce power of the federal government in its control over the expanded activities of interstate commerce, and in protecting that commerce from burdens, interferences, and conspiracies to restrain and monopolize it. But the authority of the federal government may not be pushed to such an extreme as to destroy the distinction, which the Commerce Clause itself establishes, between commerce "among the several States" and the internal concerns of a State. The same answer must be made to the contention that is based upon the serious economic situation which led to the passage of the Recovery Act - the fall in prices, the decline in wages and employment, and the curtailment of the market for commodities. Stress is laid upon the great importance of maintaining wage distributions which would provide the necessary stimulus in stating "the cumulative forces making for expanding commercial activity." Without in any way disparaging this motive, it is enough to say that the recuperative efforts of the federal government must be made in a manner consistent with the authority granted by the Constitution.

We are of the opinion that the attempt, through the provisions of the Code, to fix the hours and wages of employees of defendants in their intrastate business was not a valid exercise of federal power.

The other violations for which [Schechter Poultry was] convicted related to the making of local sales. Ten counts for violation of the provision as to "straight killing" were for permitting customers to make "selections of individual chickens taken from particular coops and half coops." Whether or not this practice is good or bad for the local trade, its effect, if any, upon interstate commerce was only indirect. The same may be said of violations of the Code by intrastate transactions consisting of the sale "of an unfit chicken" and of sales which were not in accord with the ordinances of the City of New York. The requirement of report as to prices and volumes of [Schechter Poultry's] sales was incident to the effort to control their intrastate business.

. . . . On . . . the grounds we have discussed, the attempted delegation of legislative power, and the attempted regulation of intrastate transaction which affect interstate commerce only indirectly, we hold the code provisions here in question to be invalid and that the judgment of conviction must be reversed.

The Right Of The People
To Keep And Bear Arms
The "Sawed-Off Shotgun" Case
United States v. Jack Miller

A well regulated Militia, being necessary to the security of a free State, the right of the people to keep and bear Arms, shall not be infringed.
　　　　　- The Constitution's Second Amendment (1791)

It shall be unlawful for any person [possessing certain types of firearms] to ship, carry, or deliver any [unregistered] firearm in interstate commerce.
　　　　　- The National Firearms Act (1934)

The Constitution's Second Amendment, authored by James Madison, guaranteed that "the right of the people to keep and bear arms" would not be infringed upon by the Federal Government. The Amendment was proposed on June 8, 1789 and approved, as part of the Bill of Rights, on December 15, 1791.

The United States Congress, in response to the public's outrage over the increased use of Prohibition Era "gangster weapons" (submachine guns and sawed-off shotguns), passed the National Firearms Act on June 23, 1934. The National Firearms Act, the first Federal firearms law enacted since the adoption of the Second Amendment in 1791, required the registration of certain types of firearms whenever transported across state lines.

Jack Miller was indicted in U.S. District Court for violating the National Firearms Act. The indictment charged that Miller had "unlawfully, willfully and feloniously" transported an unregistered firearm - a double-barrel 12-gauge sawed-off shotgun - between Oklahoma and Arkansas.

On January 3, 1939 the U.S. District Court, finding that the National Firearms Act was unconstitutional - a violation of the Constitution's Second Amendment - threw out the charges against Miller. The United States Justice Department appealed this decision to the United States Supreme Court.

On May 15, 1939 the 8-0 decision of the United States Supreme Court was announced by Justice James McReynolds.

The *Sawed-Off Shotgun* Court

Chief Justice Charles Evans Hughes
Appointed Chief Justice by President Hoover
Served 1930 - 1941

Associate Justice James McReynolds
Appointed by President Wilson
Served 1914 - 1941

Associate Justice Pierce Butler
Appointed by President Harding
Served 1922 - 1939

Associate Justice Harlan Fiske Stone
Appointed by President Coolidge
Served 1925 - 1946

Associate Justice Owen Roberts
Appointed by President Hoover
Served 1930 - 1945

Associate Justice Hugo Black
Appointed by President Franklin Roosevelt
Served 1937 - 1971

Associate Justice Stanley Reed
Appointed by President Franklin Roosevelt
Served 1938 - 1957

Associate Justice Felix Frankfurter
Appointed by President Franklin Roosevelt
Served 1939 - 1962

The unedited legal text of *United States v. Jack Miller* can be found in volume 307 of *United States Reports* beginning on page 174. Our edited plain-English text follows.

United States v. Jack Miller
May 15, 1939

Justice James McReynolds: An indictment in the [Arkansas] District Court charged that Jack Miller . . . "did unlawfully, knowingly, willfully, and feloniously transport in interstate commerce from [Oklahoma to Arkansas] a certain firearm, . . . a double barrel 12-gauge . . . shotgun . . . , not having registered said firearm as required by . . . the regulations issued under authority of the . . . Act of Congress known as the "National Firearms Act" approved June 26, 1934, contrary to the form of the statute in such case made and provided, and against the peace and dignity of the United States."

[Miller argued that t]he National Firearms Act is . . . an attempt to usurp police power reserved to the States, and is therefore unconstitutional. [Miller also argued that the National Firearms Act] offends the inhibition of the Second Amendment to the Constitution:

> "A well regulated militia, being necessary to the security of a free State, the right of people to keep and bear arms, shall not be infringed."

The District Court held that . . . the [National Firearms] Act violates the Second Amendment. It accordingly sustained [approved Miller's arguments] and quashed [annulled] the indictment.

. . . . In the absence of any evidence tending to show that possession or use of a "shotgun having a barrel of less than eighteen inches in length" at this time has some reasonable relationship to the preservation or efficiency of a well regulated militia, we cannot say that the Second Amendment guarantees the right to keep and bear such an instrument. Certainly it is not within judicial notice that this weapon is any part of the ordinary military equipment or that its use could contribute to the common defense.

The Constitution as originally adopted granted to the Congress power

"To provide for calling forth the militia to execute the laws of the Union, suppress insurrections and repel invasions; to provide for organizing, arming, and disciplining, the militia, and for governing such part of them as may be employed in the service of the United States, reserving to the States respectively, the appointment of the officers, and the authority of training the militia according to the discipline prescribed by Congress."

With obvious purpose to assure the continuation and render possible the effectiveness of such forces the declaration and guarantee of the Second Amendment were made. It must be interpreted and applied with that end in view.

The militia which the States were expected to maintain and train is set in contrast with troops which they were forbidden to keep without the consent of Congress. The sentiment of the time strongly disfavored standing armies; the common view was that adequate defense of country and laws could be secured though the militia - civilians primarily, soldiers on occasion.

The signification attributed to the term militia appears from the debates in the [Constitutional] Convention, the history and legislation of Colonies and States, and the writings of approved commentators. These show plainly enough that the militia comprised all males physically capable of acting in concert for the common defense. "A body of citizens enrolled for military discipline." And further, that ordinarily when called for service these men were expected to appear bearing arms supplied by themselves and of the kind in common use at the time.

Blackstone's *Commentaries* points out "that king Alfred first settled a national militia in this kingdom" and traces the subsequent development and use of such forces.

Adam Smith's *Wealth of Nations* contains an extended account of the militia. It is there said:

"Men of republican principles have been jealous of a standing army as dangerous to liberty.

"In a militia, the character of the laborer, artificer, or tradesman, predominates over that of the soldier; in a standing army, that of the soldier predominates over every other character, and in this distinction seems to consist the essential difference between those two different species of military force."

[Osgood's] *The American Colonies In The 17th Century* affirms in reference to the early system of defense in New England:

"In all the colonies, as in England, the militia system was based on the principle of the assize of arms. This implied the general obligation of all adult male inhabitants to possess arms, and, with certain exceptions, to cooperate in the work of defense.

"The possession of arms also implied the possession of ammunition, and the authorities paid quite as much attention to the latter as to the former.

"A year later [1632] it was ordered that any single man who had not furnished himself with arms might be put out to service, and this became a permanent part of the legislation of the colony [Massachusetts]."

Also

"Clauses intended to insure the possession of arms and ammunition by all who were subject to military service appear in all the important enactments concerning military affairs. Fines were the penalty for delinquency, whether of towns or individuals. According to the usage of the times, the infantry of Massachusetts consisted of pikemen and musketeers. The law, as enacted in 1649 and thereafter, provided that each of the former should be armed with a pike, corselet, head-piece, sword, and knapsack. The musketeer should carry a 'good fixed musket,' not under bastard musket bore, not less than three feet nine inches, nor more than four feet three inches in length, a priming wire, scourer, and mould, a sword, rest, bandoleers, one pound of powder, twenty bullets, and two fathoms of match. The law also required that two-thirds of each company should be musketeers."

The General Court of Massachusetts, January Session 1784, provided for the organization and government of the militia. It directed that the Train Band should "contain all able bodied men, from sixteen to forty years of age, and the Alarm List, all other men under sixty years of age, . . ." Also, "That every non-commissioned officer and private soldier of the said militia not under the control of parents, masters or guardians, and being of sufficient ability therefor in the judgment of the Selectmen of the town in which he shall dwell, shall equip himself, and be constantly provided with a good fire arm, etc."

By an Act passed April 4, 1786 the New York Legislature directed:

"That every able-bodied male person, being a citizen of this State, or of any of the United States, and residing in this State, (except such persons as are herein after excepted) and who are of the age of sixteen, and under the age of forty-five years, shall, by the Captain or commanding Officer of the Beat in which such citizens shall reside, within four months after the passing of this Act, be enrolled in the Company of such Beat. . . . That every citizen so enrolled and notified, shall, within three months thereafter, provide himself, at his own expense, with a good musket or firelock, a sufficient bayonet and belt, a pouch with a box therein to contain not less than twenty-four cartridges suited to the bore of his musket or firelock, each cartridge containing a proper quantity of powder and ball, two spare flints, a blanket and knapsack; . . ."

The General Assembly of Virginia, October, 1785, declared, "The defense and safety of the Commonwealth depend upon having its citizens properly armed and taught the knowledge of military duty."

It further provided for organization and control of the militia and directed that "All free male persons between the ages of eighteen and fifty years," with certain exceptions, "shall be enrolled or formed into companies." "There shall be a private muster of every company once in two months."

Also that

"Every officer and soldier shall appear at his respective muster-field on the day appointed, by eleven o'clock in the forenoon, armed, equipped, and accoutred, as follows: . . . every non-commissioned officer and private with a good, clean musket carrying an ounce ball, and three feet eight inches long in the barrel, with a good bayonet and iron ramrod well fitted thereto, a cartridge box properly made, to contain and secure twenty cartridges fitted to his musket, a good knapsack and canteen, and moreover, each non-commissioned officer and private shall have at every muster one pound of good powder, and four pounds of lead, including twenty blind cartridges; and each serjeant shall have a pair of moulds fit to cast balls for their respective companies, to be purchased by the commanding officer out of the monies arising on delinquencies. Provided, that the militia of the counties westward of the Blue Ridge, and the counties below adjoining thereto, shall not be obliged to be armed with muskets, but may have good rifles with proper accoutrements, in lieu thereof. And every of the said officers, non-commissioned officers, and privates, shall constantly keep the aforesaid arms, accoutrements, and ammunition, ready to be produced whenever called for by his commanding officer. If any private shall make it appear to the satisfaction of the court hereafter to be appointed for trying delinquencies under this act that he is so poor that he cannot purchase the arms herein required, such court shall cause them to be purchased out of the money arising from delinquents."

Most if not all of the States have adopted provisions touching the right to keep and bear arms. Differences in the language employed in these have naturally led to somewhat variant conclusions concerning the scope of the right guaranteed. But none of them seem to afford any material support for the challenged ruling of the court below [the District Court].

. . . . We are unable to accept the conclusion of the court below and the challenged judgment must be reversed. The cause will be remanded [returned to the lower court] for further proceedings.

The Law Of War
A Japanese War Criminal
Appeals His Death Sentence
In The Matter Of General Tomoyuki Yamashita

Stern justice shall be meted out to all war criminals.
- The Potsdam Declaration, July 26, 1945

On September 2, 1945 (V-J Day) Japan surrendered to end the Second World War. The next day Tomoyuki Yamashita, Commanding General of the Imperial Japanese Army in the Philippines, surrendered his Army and became a prisoner of war. Ten days later President Truman and the Joint Chiefs of Staff instructed General Douglas MacArthur, Commander of the Pacific Forces, to prosecute Japanese war criminals under the law of war - international agreements, including the Geneva Convention, which called for punishments for criminal actions perpetrated by individuals and those under their command during wartime.

General Yamashita, known as "The Tiger of Malaya" for a 1942 Japanese military victory, was charged on October 8, 1945 with multiple violations of the law of war. The charges against Yamashita alleged that while commander of the Japanese Army in the Philippines, October 9, 1944 through September 2, 1945, he permitted his soldiers to commit atrocities against Philippine civilian and American prisoners of war, causing between 60,000 and 100,000 deaths.

The trial of General Tomoyuki Yamashita, held in Manila before a military tribunal, began on October 29, 1945 and heard 286 witnesses and took over 3,000 pages of testimony, before concluding on December 7, 1945. Yamashita was found guilty of war crimes and sentenced to death by hanging. Yamashita's defenders argued that the death sentence had been "imposed in thoughtless haste," "without regard for due process of law," and in a "spirit of revenge and retribution" which constituted a "legalized lynching." Yamashita appealed to the United States Supreme Court.

On February 4, 1946 the 7-2 decision of the U.S. Supreme Court was announced by Chief Justice Harlan Fiske Stone.

The *Yamashita* Court

Chief Justice Harlan Fiske Stone
Appointed Chief Justice by President Franklin Roosevelt
Served 1925 - 1946

Associate Justice Hugo Black
Appointed by President Franklin Roosevelt
Served 1937 - 1971

Associate Justice Stanley Reed
Appointed by President Franklin Roosevelt
Served 1938 - 1957

Associate Justice Felix Frankfurter
Appointed by President Franklin Roosevelt
Served 1939 - 1962

Associate Justice William O. Douglas
Appointed by President Franklin Roosevelt
Served 1939 - 1975

Associate Justice Frank Murphy
Appointed by President Franklin Roosevelt
Served 1940 - 1949

Associate Justice Robert Jackson
Appointed by President Franklin Roosevelt
Served 1941 - 1954

Associate Justice Wiley Rutledge
Appointed by President Franklin Roosevelt
Served 1943 - 1949

Associate Justice Harold Burton
Appointed by President Truman
Served 1945 - 1958

The unedited legal text of *In The Matter of General Tomoyuki Yamashita* can be found in volume 327 of *United States Reports* beginning on page 1. Our edited plain-English text follows.

In The Matter Of General Tomoyuki Yamashita February 4, 1946

Chief Justice Harlan Fiske Stone: . . . . [Tomoyuki Yamashita] was the Commanding General of the Fourteenth Army Group of the Imperial Japanese Army in the Philippine Islands. [On September 3, 1945] he surrendered to and became a prisoner of war of the United States Army. . . . On September 25th, by order of [Lieutenant General Styer], Commanding General of the United States Army Forces, Western Pacific, which command embraces the Philippine Islands, [General Yamashita] was served with a charge prepared by the Judge Advocate General's Department of the Army, [charging General Yamashita] with a violation of the law of war. On October 8, 1945, [General Yamashita], after pleading not guilty to the charge, was held for trial before a military commission of five Army officers appointed by order of General Styer. . . .

The trial then proceeded until its conclusion on December 7, 1945, the commission hearing two hundred and eighty-six witnesses, who gave over three thousand pages of testimony. On that date [General Yamashita] was found guilty of the offense as charged and sentenced to death by hanging.

The petitions for [the release of Yamashita claimed that] the purpose of the trial was unlawful for reasons which are now urged as showing that the military commission was without lawful authority or jurisdiction [legal right] to place [Yamashita] on trial, as follows:

(a) That the military commission which tried and convicted [General Yamashita] was not lawfully created, and that no military commission to try [him] for violations of the law of war could lawfully be convened after the cessation of hostilities between the armed forces of the United States and Japan;

(b) that the charge preferred against [Yamashita] fails to charge him with a violation of the law of war;

(c) that the commission was without authority and jurisdiction to try and convict [Yamashita] because the order governing the procedure of the commission permitted the admission in evidence of depositions [sworn testimony], affidavits [written statements of facts, sworn to by their author] and hearsay [second-hand testimony] and opinion evidence, and because the commission's rulings admitting such evidence were in violation of the 25th and 38th Articles of War and the Geneva Convention, and deprived [Yamashita] of a fair trial in violation of the Due Process Clause of the Fifth Amendment;

(d) that the commission was without authority and jurisdiction in the premises because of the failure to give advance notice of [General Yamashita]'s trial to the neutral power representing the interests of Japan as a belligerent as required by Article 60 of the Geneva Convention.

. . . . The Supreme Court of the Philippine Islands, after hearing argument, denied the petition . . . on the ground, among others, that its jurisdiction was limited to an inquiry as to the jurisdiction of the commission to place [Yamashita] on trial for the offense charged, and that the commission, being validly constituted by the order of General Styer, had jurisdiction over the person of [General Yamashita] and over the trial for the offense charged.

. . . . In a proclamation of July 2, 1942 [President Franklin Roosevelt] proclaimed that enemy belligerents who, during time of war, enter the United States, or any territory or possession thereof, and who violate the law of war, should be subject to the law of war and to the jurisdiction of military tribunals. Paragraph 10 of the Declaration of Potsdam of July 26, 1945, declared that " . . . stern justice shall be meted out to all war criminals including those who have visited cruelties upon prisoners." This Declaration was accepted by the Japanese government by its note of August 10, 1945.

By direction of the President, the Joint Chiefs of Staff of the American Military Forces, on September 12, 1945, instructed General [Douglas] MacArthur, Commander-in-Chief, United States Army Forces, Pacific, to proceed with the trial, before appropriate military tribunals, of such Japanese war criminals "as have been or may be apprehended." By order of General MacArthur of September 24, 1945, General Styer was specifically directed to proceed with the trial of [Yamashita] upon the charge here involved. This order was accompanied by detailed rules and regulations which General MacArthur prescribed for the trial of war criminals. These regulations directed, among other things, that review of the sentence imposed by the commission should be by the officer convening it, with "authority to approve, mitigate [lessen], remit [annul], commute [change], suspend, reduce or otherwise alter the sentence imposed," and directed that no sentence of death should be carried into effect until confirmed by the Commander-in-Chief, United States Army Forces, Pacific.

It thus appears that the order creating the commission for the trial of [Yamashita] was authorized by military command, and was in complete conformity to the Act of Congress sanctioning the creation of such tribunals for the trial of offenses against the law of war committed by enemy combatants. [W]e turn to the question whether the authority to create the commission and direct the trial by military order continued after the cessation of hostilities.

An important incident to the conduct of war is the adoption of measures by the military commander, not only to repel and defeat the enemy, but to seize and subject to disciplinary measures those enemies who, in their attempt to thwart or impede our military effort, have violated the law of war. The trial and punishment of enemy combatants who have committed violations of the law of war is thus not only a part of the conduct of war operating as a preventive measure against such violations, but is an exercise of the authority sanctioned by Congress to administer the system of military justice recognized by the law of war. That sanction is without qualification as to the exercise of this authority so long as a state of war exists - from its declaration until peace is proclaimed. The war power, from which the commission derives its existence, is not limited to victories in the field, but carries with it the inherent power to guard against the immediate renewal of the conflict, and to remedy, at least in ways Congress has recognized, the evils which the military operations have produced.

We cannot say that there is no authority to convene a commission after hostilities have ended to try violations of the law of war committed before their cessation, at least until peace has been officially recognized by treaty or proclamation of the political branch of the Government. In fact, in most instances the practical administration of the system of military justice under the law of war would fail if such authority were thought to end with the cessation of hostilities. For only after their cessation could the greater number of offenders and the principal ones be apprehended and subjected to trial.

No writer on international law appears to have regarded the power of military tribunals, otherwise competent to try violations of the law of war, as terminating before the formal state of war has ended.

In our own military history there have been numerous instances in which offenders were tried by military commission after the cessation of hostilities and before the proclamation of peace, for offenses against the law of war committed before the cessation of hostilities.

The extent to which the power to prosecute violations of the law of war shall be exercised before peace is declared rests, not with the courts, but with the political branch of the Government, and may itself be governed by the terms of an armistice or the treaty of peace. Here, peace has not been agreed upon or proclaimed. Japan, by her acceptance of the Potsdam Declaration and her surrender, has acquiesced in the trials of those guilty of violations of the law of war. The conduct of the trial by the military commission has been authorized by the political branch of the Government, by military command, by international law and usage, and by the terms of the surrender of the Japanese government.

Neither Congressional action nor the military orders constituting the commission authorized it to place [Yamashita] on trial unless the charge preferred against him is of a violation of the law of war. The charge, so far as now relevant, is that [Yamashita], between October 9, 1944 and September 2, 1945, in the Philippine Islands, "while commander of armed forces of Japan at war with the United States of America and its allies, unlawfully disregarded and failed to discharge his duty as commander to control the operations of the members of his command, permitting them to commit brutal atrocities and other high crimes against people of the United States and of its allies and dependencies, particularly the Philippines; and he thereby violated the laws of war." . . .

Bills of particulars [statements of the charges], filed by the prosecution by order of the commission, allege a series of acts, one hundred and twenty-three in number, committed by members of the forces under [General Yamashita]'s command during the period mentioned. The first item specifies the execution of "a deliberate plan and purpose to massacre and exterminate a large part of the civilian population of Batangas Province, and to devastate and destroy public, private and religious property therein, as a result of which more than 25,000 men, women and children, all unarmed noncombatant civilians, were brutally mistreated and killed, without cause or trial, and entire settlements were devastated and destroyed wantonly and without military necessity." Other items specify acts of violence, cruelty and homicide inflicted upon the civilian population and prisoners of war, acts of wholesale pillage and the wanton destruction of religious monuments.

It is not denied that such acts directed against the civilian population of an occupied country and against prisoners of war are recognized in international law as violations of the law of war. But it is urged that the charge does not allege that [General Yamashita] has either committed or directed the commission of such acts, and consequently that no violation is charged as against him. But this overlooks the fact that the gist of the charge is an unlawful breach of duty by [Yamashita] as an army commander to control the operations of the members of his command by "permitting them to commit" the extensive and widespread atrocities specified. The question then is whether the law of war imposes on an army commander a duty to take such appropriate measures as are within his power to control the troops under his command for the prevention of the specified acts which are violations of the law of war and which are likely to attend the occupation of hostile territory by an uncontrolled soldiery, and whether he may be charged with personal responsibility for his failure to take such measures when violations result. That this was the precise issue to be tried was made clear by the statement of the prosecution at the opening of the trial.

It is evident that the conduct of military operations by troops whose excesses are unrestrained by the orders or efforts of their commander would almost certainly result in violations which it is the purpose of the law of war to prevent. Its purpose to protect civilian populations and prisoners of war from brutality would largely be defeated if the commander of an invading army could with impunity neglect to take reasonable measures for their protection. Hence the law of war presupposes that its violation is to be avoided through the control of the operations of war by commanders who are to some extent responsible for their subordinates.

. . . . We do not make the laws of war but we respect them so far as they do not conflict with the commands of Congress or the Constitution. There is no contention that the present charge, thus read, is without the support of evidence, or that the commission held [Yamashita] responsible for failing to take measures which were beyond his control or inappropriate for a commanding officer to take in the circumstances. We do not here appraise the evidence on which [Yamashita] was convicted. We do not consider what measures, if any, [General Yamashita] took to prevent the commission, by the troops under his command, of the plain violations of the law of war detailed in the bill of particulars, or whether such measures as he may have taken were appropriate and sufficient to discharge the duty imposed upon him. These are questions within the peculiar competence of the military officers composing the commission and were for it to decide. It is plain that the charge on which [General Yamashita] was tried charged him with a breach of his duty to control the operations of the members of his command, by permitting them to commit the specified atrocities. This was enough to require the commission to hear evidence tending to establish the culpable failure of [Yamashita] to perform the duty imposed on him by the law of war and to pass upon its sufficiency to establish guilt.

. . . . We cannot say that the commission, in admitting evidence to which objection is now made, violated any act of Congress, treaty or military command defining the commission's authority. For reasons already stated we hold that the commission's rulings on evidence and on the mode of conducting these proceedings against [General Yamashita] are not reviewable by the courts, but only by the reviewing military authorities. From this viewpoint it is unnecessary to consider what, in other situations, the Fifth Amendment might require, and as to that no intimation one way or the other is to be implied. Nothing we have said is to be taken as indicating any opinion on the question of the wisdom of considering such evidence, or whether the action of a military tribunal in admitting evidence, which Congress or controlling military command has directed to be excluded, may be drawn in question. . . .

Article 60 of the Geneva Convention of July 27, 1929 to which the United States and Japan were signatories, provides that "At the opening of a judicial proceeding directed against a prisoner of war, the detaining Power shall advise the representative of the protecting Power thereof as soon as possible, and always before the date set for the opening of the trial." [Yamashita] relies on the failure to give the prescribed notice to the protecting power to establish want of authority in the commission to proceed with the trial.

For reasons already stated we conclude that Article 60 of the Geneva Convention . . . applies only to persons who are subjected to judicial proceedings for offenses committed while prisoners of war.

It thus appears that the order convening the commission was a lawful order, that the Commission was lawfully constituted, that [Yamashita] was charged with violation of the law of war, and that the commission had authority to proceed with the trial, and in doing so did not violate any military, statutory or constitutional command. . . . We therefore conclude that the detention of [Yamashita] for trial and his detention upon his conviction, subject to the prescribed review by the military authorities, were lawful. . . .

Justice Frank Murphy, dissenting: The significance of the issue facing the Court today cannot be over emphasized. An American military commission has been established to try a fallen military commander of a conquered nation for an alleged war crime. The authority for such action grows out of the exercise of the power conferred upon Congress by Article 1, Section 8, Clause 10 of the Constitution to "define and punish . . . offenses against the law of nations. . . ." The grave issue raised by this case is whether a military commission so established and so authorized may disregard the procedural rights of an accused person as guaranteed by the Constitution, especially by the Due Process Clause of the Fifth Amendment.

The answer is plain. The Fifth Amendment guarantee of due process of law applies to "any person" who is accused of a crime by the Federal Government or any of its agencies. No exception is made as to those who are accused of war crimes or as to those who possess the status of an enemy belligerent. Indeed, such an exception would be contrary to the whole philosophy of human rights which makes the Constitution the great living document that it is. The immutable rights of the individual, including those secured by the Due Process Clause of the Fifth Amendment, belong not alone to the members of those nations that excel on the battlefield or that subscribe to the democratic ideology. They belong to every person in the world, victor or vanquished, whatever may be his race, color or beliefs. They rise above any status of belligerency or outlawry. They survive any popular passion or frenzy of the moment. No court or legislature or executive, not even the mightiest army in the world, can ever destroy them. Such is the universal and indestructible nature of the rights which the Due Process Clause of the Fifth Amendment recognizes and protects when life or liberty is threatened by virtue of the authority of the United States.

The existence of these rights, unfortunately, is not always respected. They are often trampled under by those who are motivated by hatred, aggression or fear. But in this nation individual rights are recognized and protected, at least in regard to governmental action. They cannot be ignored by any branch of the Government, even the military, except under the most extreme and urgent circumstances.

The failure of the military commission to obey the dictates of the due process requirements of the Fifth Amendment is apparent in this case. The petitioner [person appealing the lower court's decision] was the commander of an army totally destroyed by the superior power of this nation. While under heavy and destructive attack by our forces, his troops committed many brutal atrocities and other high crimes. Hostilities ceased and he voluntarily surrendered. At that point he was entitled, as an individual protected by the Due Process Clause of the Fifth Amendment, to be treated fairly and justly according to the accepted rules of law and procedure. He was also entitled to a fair trial as to any alleged crimes and to be free from charges of legally unrecognized crimes that would serve only to permit his accusers to satisfy their desires for revenge.

A military commission was appointed to try [Yamashita] for an alleged war crime. The trial was ordered to be held in territory over which the United States has complete sovereignty. No military necessity or other emergency demanded the suspension of the safeguards of due process. Yet [General Yamashita] was rushed to trial under an improper charge, given insufficient time to prepare an adequate defense, deprived of the benefits of some of the most elementary rules of evidence and summarily sentenced to be hanged. In all this needless and unseemly haste there was no serious attempt to charge or to prove that he committed a recognized violation of the laws of war. He was not charged with personally participating in the acts of atrocity or with ordering or condoning their commission. Not even knowledge of these crimes was attributed to him. It was simply alleged that he unlawfully disregarded and failed to discharge his duty as commander to control the operations of the members of his command, permitting them to commit the acts of atrocity. The recorded annals of warfare and the established principles of international law afford not the slightest precedent [previous decision] for such a charge. This indictment [charge] in effect permitted the military commission to make the crime whatever it willed, dependent upon its biased view as to [Yamashita]'s duties and his disregard thereof, a practice reminiscent of that pursued in certain less respected nations in recent years.

In my opinion, such a procedure is unworthy of the traditions of our people or of the immense sacrifices that they have made to advance the common ideals of mankind. The high feelings of the moment doubtless will be satisfied. But in the sober afterglow will come the realization of the boundless and dangerous implications of the procedure sanctioned today. No one in a position of command in an army, from sergeant to general, can escape those implications. Indeed, the fate of some future President of the United States and his chiefs of staff and military advisers may well have been sealed by this decision. But even more significant will be the hatred and ill-will growing out of the application of this unprecedented procedure. That has been the inevitable effect of every method of punishment disregarding the element of personal culpability. The effect in this instance, unfortunately, will be magnified infinitely for here we are dealing with the rights of man on an international level. To subject an enemy belligerent to an unfair trial, to charge him with an unrecognized crime, or to vent on him our retributive emotions only antagonizes the enemy nation and hinders the reconciliation necessary to a peaceful world.

That there were brutal atrocities inflicted upon the helpless Filipino people, to whom tyranny is no stranger, by Japanese armed forces under [Yamashita]'s command is undeniable. Starvation, execution or massacre without trial, torture, rape, murder and wanton destruction of property were foremost among the outright violations of the laws of war and of the conscience of a civilized world. That just punishment should be meted out to all those responsible for criminal acts of this nature is also beyond dispute. But these factors do not answer the problem in this case. They do not justify the abandonment of our devotion to justice in dealing with a fallen enemy commander. To conclude otherwise is to admit that the enemy has lost the battle but has destroyed our ideals.

War breeds atrocities. From the earliest conflicts of recorded history to the global struggles of modern times inhumanities, lust and pillage have been the inevitable byproducts of man's resort to force and arms. Unfortunately, such despicable acts have a dangerous tendency to call forth primitive impulses of vengeance and retaliation among the victimized peoples. The satisfaction of such impulses in turn breeds resentment and fresh tension. Thus does the spiral of cruelty and hatred grow.

If we are ever to develop an orderly international community based upon a recognition of human dignity it is of the utmost importance that the necessary punishment of those guilty of atrocities be as free as possible from the ugly stigma of revenge and vindictiveness. Justice must be tempered by compassion rather than by vengeance. In this, the first case involving this momentous problem ever to reach this Court, our responsibility is both lofty and difficult. We must insist, within the confines of our proper jurisdiction [legal right], that the highest standards of justice be applied in this trial of an enemy commander conducted under the authority of the United States. Otherwise stark retribution will be free to masquerade in a cloak of false legalism. And the hatred and cynicism engendered by that retribution will supplant the great ideals to which this nation is dedicated.

This Court fortunately has taken the first and most important step toward insuring the supremacy of law and justice in the treatment of an enemy belligerent accused of violating the laws of war. Jurisdiction properly has been asserted to inquire "into the cause of restraint of liberty" of such a person. Thus the obnoxious doctrine asserted by the Government in this case, to the effect that restraints of liberty resulting from military trials of war criminals are political matters completely outside the arena of judicial review, has been rejected fully and unquestionably. . . .

[F]or the purposes of this case I accept the scope of review recognized by the Court at this time. As I understand it, the following issues in connection with war criminal trials are reviewable through the use of the writ of habeas corpus [an order to appear before a judge]: (1) whether the military commission was lawfully created and had authority to try and to convict the accused of a war crime; (2) whether the charge against the accused stated a violation of the laws of war; (3) whether the commission, in admitting certain evidence, violated any law or military command defining the commission's authority in that respect; and (4) whether the commission lacked jurisdiction because of a failure to give advance notice to the protecting power as required by treaty or convention.

The Court, in my judgment, demonstrates conclusively that the military commission was lawfully created in this instance and that [Yamashita] could not object to its power to try him for a recognized war crime. Without pausing here to discuss the third and fourth issues, however, I find it impossible to agree that the charge against [Yamashita] stated a recognized violation of the laws of war.

It is important, in the first place, to appreciate the background of events preceding this trial. From October 9, 1944, to September 2, 1945, [Yamashita] was the Commanding General of the 14th Army Group of the Imperial Japanese Army, with headquarters in the Philippines. The reconquest of the Philippines by the armed forces of the United States began approximately at the time when [Yamashita] assumed this command. Combined with a great and decisive sea battle, an invasion was made on the island of Leyte on October 20, 1944. "In the six days of the great naval action the Japanese position in the Philippines had become extremely critical. Most of the serviceable elements of the Japanese Navy had been committed to the battle with disastrous results. The strike had miscarried, and General MacArthur's land wedge was firmly implanted in the vulnerable flank of the enemy. . . . There were 260,000 Japanese troops scattered over the Philippines but most of them might as well have been on the other side of the world so far as the enemy's ability to shift them to meet the American thrusts was concerned. If General MacArthur succeeded in establishing himself in the Visayas where he could stage, exploit, and spread under cover of overwhelming naval and air superiority, nothing could prevent him from overrunning the Philippines."

By the end of 1944 the island of Leyte was largely in American hands. And on January 9, 1945, the island of Luzon was invaded.

"Yamashita's inability to cope with General MacArthur's swift moves, his desired reaction to the deception measures, the guerrillas, and General Kenney's aircraft combined to place the Japanese in an impossible situation. The enemy was forced into a piecemeal commitment of his troops."

It was at this time and place that most of the alleged atrocities took place. Organized resistance around Manila ceased on February 23. Repeated land and air assaults pulverized the enemy and within a few months there was little left of [Yamashita]'s command except a few remnants which had gathered for a last stand among the precipitous mountains.

As the military commission here noted,

"The Defense established the difficulties faced by the accused with respect not only to the swift and overpowering advance of American forces, but also to the errors of his predecessors, weaknesses in organization, equipment, supply with especial reference to food and gasoline, training, communication, discipline and morale of his troops. It was alleged that the sudden assignment of Naval and Air Forces to his tactical command presented almost insurmountable difficulties. This situation was followed, the defense contended, by failure to obey his orders to withdraw troops from Manila, and the subsequent massacre of unarmed civilians, particularly by Naval forces. Prior to the Luzon Campaign, Naval forces had reported to a separate ministry in the Japanese Government and Naval Commanders may not have been receptive or experienced in this instance with respect to a joint land operation under a single commander who was designated from the Army Service."

The day of final reckoning for the enemy arrived in August, 1945. On September 3, [Yamashita] surrendered to the United States Army at Baguio, Luzon. He immediately became a prisoner of war and was interned in prison in conformity with the rules of international law. On September 25, approximately three weeks after surrendering, he was served with the charge in issue in this case. Upon service of the charge he was removed from the status of a prisoner of war and placed in confinement as an accused war criminal. Arraignment [court proceeding charging an individual and calling for a plea as to guilt or innocence] followed on October 8 before a military commission specially appointed for the case. [Yamashita] pleaded not guilty. He was also served on that day with a bill of particulars [statement of charges] alleging sixty-four crimes by troops under his command. A supplemental bill alleging fifty-nine more crimes by his troops was filed on October 29, the same day that the trial began. No continuance [postponement] was allowed for preparation of a defense as to the supplemental bill. The trial continued uninterrupted until December 5, 1945. On December 7 [Yamashita] was found guilty as charged and was sentenced to be hanged.

[Yamashita] was accused of having "unlawfully disregarded and failed to discharge his duty as commander to control the operations of the members of his command, permitting them to commit brutal atrocities and other high crimes." The bills of particular further alleged that specific acts of atrocity were committed by "members of the armed forces of Japan under the command of the accused." Nowhere was it alleged that [Yamashita] personally committed any of the atrocities, or that he ordered their commission, or that he had any knowledge of the commission thereof by members of his command.

The findings of the military commission bear out this absence of any direct personal charge against [Yamashita]. The commission merely found that atrocities and other high crimes "have been committed by members of the Japanese armed forces under your command . . . that they were not sporadic in nature but in many cases were methodically supervised by Japanese officers and noncommissioned officers . . . that during the period in question you failed to provide effective control of your troops as was required by the circumstances."

In other words, read against the background of military events in the Philippines subsequent to October 9, 1944, these charges amount to this:

"We, the victorious American forces, have done everything possible to destroy and disorganize your lines of communication, your effective control of your personnel, your ability to wage war. In those respects we have succeeded. We have defeated and crushed your forces. And now we charge and condemn you for having been inefficient in maintaining control of your troops during the period when we were so effectively besieging and eliminating your forces and blocking your ability to maintain effective control. Many terrible atrocities were committed by your disorganized troops. Because these atrocities were so widespread we will not bother to charge or prove that you committed, ordered or condoned any of them. We will assume that they must have resulted from your inefficiency and negligence as a commander. In short, we charge you with the crime of inefficiency in controlling your troops. We will judge the discharge of your duties by the disorganization which we ourselves created in large part. Our standards of judgment are whatever we wish to make them."

Nothing in all history or in international law, at least as far as I am aware, justifies such a charge against a fallen commander of a defeated force. To use the very inefficiency and disorganization created by the victorious forces as the primary basis for condemning officers of the defeated armies bears no resemblance to justice or to military reality.

International law makes no attempt to define the duties of a commander of an army under constant and overwhelming assault; nor does it impose liability under such circumstances for failure to meet the ordinary responsibilities of command. The omission is understandable. Duties, as well as ability to control troops, vary according to the nature and intensity of the particular battle. To find an unlawful deviation from duty under battle conditions requires difficult and speculative calculations. Such calculations become highly untrustworthy when they are made by the victor in relation to the actions of a vanquished commander. Objective and realistic norms of conduct are then extremely unlikely to be used in forming a judgment as to deviations from duty. The probability that vengeance will form the major part of the victor's judgment is an unfortunate but inescapable fact. So great is that probability that international law refuses to recognize such a judgment as a basis for a war crime, however fair the judgment may be in a particular instance. It is this consideration that undermines the charge against [Yamashita]. The indictment permits, indeed compels, the military commission of a victorious nation to sit in judgment upon the military strategy and actions of the defeated enemy and to use its conclusions to determine the criminal liability of an enemy commander. Life and liberty are made to depend upon the biased will of the victor rather than upon objective standards of conduct.

The Court's reliance upon vague and indefinite references in certain of the Hague Conventions and the Geneva Red

Cross Convention is misplaced. Thus the statement in Article 1 of the Annex to Hague Convention (October 18, 1907) to the effect that the laws, rights and duties of war apply to military and volunteer corps only if they are "commanded by a person responsible for his subordinates," has no bearing upon the problem in this case. Even if it has, the clause "responsible for his subordinates" fails to state to whom the responsibility is owed or to indicate the type of responsibility contemplated. The phrase has received differing interpretations by authorities on international law. . . .

The provisions of the other conventions referred to by the Court are on their face equally devoid of relevance or significance to the situation here in issue. Neither Article 19 of [the] Hague Convention nor Article 26 of the Geneva Red Cross Convention of 1929 refers to circumstances where the troops of a commander commit atrocities while under heavily adverse battle conditions. Reference is also made to the requirement of Article 43 of the Annex to Hague Convention that the commander of a force occupying enemy territory "shall take all the measures in his power to restore, and ensure, as far as possible, public order and safety, while respecting, unless absolutely prevented, the laws in force in the country." But [Yamashita] was more than a commander of a force occupying enemy territory. He was the leader of an army under constant and devastating attacks by a superior re-invading force. This provision is silent as to the responsibilities of a commander under such conditions as that.

Even the laws of war heretofore recognized by this nation fail to impute responsibility to a fallen commander for excesses committed by his disorganized troops while under attack. Paragraph 347 of the [U.S.] War Department publication, *Basic Field Manual, Rules of Land Warfare*, states the principal offenses under the laws of war recognized by the

United States. This includes all of the atrocities which the Japanese troops were alleged to have committed in this instance.

. . . . There are numerous instances, especially with reference to the Philippine Insurrection in 1900 and 1901, where commanding officers were found to have violated the laws of war by specifically ordering members of their command to commit atrocities and other war crimes. And in other cases officers have been held liable where they knew that a crime was to be committed, had the power to prevent it and failed to exercise that power. In no recorded instance, however, has the mere inability to control troops under fire or attack by superior forces been made the basis of a charge of violating the laws of war.

The Government claims that the principle that commanders in the field are bound to control their troops has been applied so as to impose liability on the United States in international arbitrations. The difference between arbitrating property rights and charging an individual with a crime against the laws of war is too obvious to require elaboration. But even more significant is the fact that even these arbitration cases fail to establish any principle of liability where troops are under constant assault and demoralizing influences by attacking forces. The same observation applies to the common law [that established by custom and usage] and statutory doctrine, referred to by the Government, that one who is under a legal duty to take protective or preventive action is guilty of criminal homicide if he willfully or negligently omits to act and death is proximately caused. No one denies that inaction or negligence may give rise to liability, civil or criminal. But it is quite another thing to say that the inability to control troops under highly competitive and disastrous battle conditions renders one guilty of a war crime in the absence of personal culpability. Had there been some element of knowledge or direct connection with the atrocities the problem would be entirely different. . . . [W]e are concerned with a proceeding involving an international crime, the treatment of which may have untold effects upon the future peace of the world. . . .

The only conclusion I can draw is that the charge made against [Yamashita] is clearly without precedent in international law or in the annals of recorded military history. This is not to say that enemy commanders may escape punishment for clear and unlawful failures to prevent atrocities. But that punishment should be based upon charges fairly drawn in light of established rules of international law and recognized concepts of justice.

But the charge in this case, as previously noted, was speedily drawn and filed but three weeks after [Yamashita] surrendered. The trial proceeded with great dispatch without allowing the defense time to prepare an adequate case. [General Yamashita]'s rights under the Due Process Clause of the Fifth Amendment were grossly and openly violated without any justification. All of this was done without any thorough investigation and prosecution of those immediately responsible for the atrocities, out of which might have come some proof or indication of personal culpability on [Yamashita]'s part. Instead the loose charge was made that great numbers of atrocities had been committed and that [Yamashita] was the commanding officer; hence he must have been guilty of disregard of duty. Under that charge the commission was free to establish whatever standard of duty on [Yamashita]'s part that it desired. By this flexible method a victorious nation may convict and execute any or all leaders of a vanquished foe, depending upon the prevailing degree of vengeance and the absence of any objective judicial review.

At a time like this when emotions are understandably high it is difficult to adopt a dispassionate attitude toward a case of this nature. Yet now is precisely the time when that attitude is most essential. While peoples in other lands may not share our beliefs as to due process and the dignity of the individual, we are not free to give effect to our emotions in reckless disregard of the rights of others. We live under the Constitution, which is the embodiment of all the high hopes and aspirations of the new world. And it is applicable in both war and peace. We must act accordingly. Indeed, an uncurbed spirit of revenge and retribution, masked in formal legal procedure for purposes of dealing with a fallen enemy commander, can do more lasting harm than all of the atrocities giving rise to that spirit. The people's faith in the fairness and objectiveness of the law can be seriously undercut by that spirit. The fires of nationalism can be further kindled. And the hearts of all mankind can be embittered and filled with hatred, leaving forlorn and impoverished the noble ideal of malice toward none and charity to all. These are the reasons that lead me to dissent in these terms.

Un-American Activities
"Are you now, or have you ever been, a member of the Communist Party?"
John T. Watkins v. United States

The House Committee on Un-American Activities believes itself com-manded to expose people and organizations attempting to destroy this country.
> - From The House Un-American Activities Committee's *100 Things You Should Known About Communism* (1951)

The House Un-American Activities Committee (1938-1975) was created to investigate subversive efforts to overthrow the United States Government. "While Congress," the Un-American Activities Committee declared, "does not have to power to deny to citizens the right to believe in, teach, or advocate, Communism, Fascism, or Nazism, it does have the right to focus the spotlight of publicity upon their activities."

On April 29, 1954 John T. Watkins, a labor union official suspected of Communist Party affiliation, was placed in the Committee's spotlight. Subpoenaed to appear before the Committee, Watkins was asked: "Are you now, or have you ever been, a member of the Communist Party?" Watkins denied Communist Party membership. He was then read a list of names of others suspected of Communist Party affiliation and asked to identify those individuals who, to his knowledge, were then or had in the past been Communist Party members. Watkins refused to answer the question, stating: "I do not believe that this Committee has the right to undertake the exposure of persons because of their past activities. . . . Until and unless a court of law so holds and directs me to answer, I most firmly refuse to discuss the political activities of my past associates."

Watkins, for his refusal to answer the Committee's questions, was tried and convicted in U.S. District Court for criminal contempt of Congress. The U.S. Court of Appeals upheld the conviction. John T. Watkins appealed to the United States Supreme Court.

On June 17, 1957 the 6-1 decision of the United States Supreme Court was announced by Chief Justice Earl Warren.

The *Un-American Activities* Court

Chief Justice Earl Warren
Appointed Chief Justice by President Eisenhower
Served 1953 - 1969

Associate Justice Hugo Black
Appointed by President Franklin Roosevelt
Served 1937 - 1971

Associate Justice Felix Frankfurter
Appointed by President Franklin Roosevelt
Served 1939 - 1962

Associate Justice William O. Douglas
Appointed by President Franklin Roosevelt
Served 1939 - 1975

Associate Justice Tom Clark
Appointed by President Truman
Served 1949 - 1967

Associate Justice John Marshall Harlan
Appointed by President Eisenhower
Served 1955 - 1971

Associate Justice William Brennan
Appointed by President Eisenhower
Served 1956 - 1990

The unedited legal text of *John T. Watkins v. United States* can be found in volume 354 of *United States Reports* beginning on page 178. Our edited plain-English text follows.

John T. Watkins v. United States
June 17, 1957

Chief Justice Earl Warren: This is a review . . . of a conviction
. . . for "contempt of Congress." The misdemeanor [petty
offense] is alleged to have been committed during a hearing
before a congressional investigating committee. It is not the
case of a truculent or contumacious witness who refuses to
answer all questions or who, by boisterous or discourteous
conduct, disturbs the decorum of the committee room.
[John T. Watkins] was prosecuted for refusing to make certain disclosures which he asserted to be beyond the authority of the committee to demand. The controversy thus
rests upon fundamental principles of the power of the
Congress and the limitations upon that power. We approach the questions presented with conscious awareness
of the far-reaching ramifications that can follow from a decision of this nature.

On April 29, 1954, [Watkins] appeared as a witness in compliance with a subpoena [order to give testimony] issued by
a Subcommittee of the Committee on Un-American Activities of the House of Representatives. The Subcommittee elicited from [Watkins] a description of his background in labor union activities. He had been an employee
of the International Harvester Company between 1935 and
1953. During the last eleven of those years, he had been on
leave of absence to serve as an official of the Farm Equipment Workers International Union, later merged into the
United Electrical, Radio and Machine Workers. He rose to
the position of President of District No. 2 of the Farm
Equipment Workers, a district defined geographically to
include generally Canton and Rock Falls, Illinois, and Du-
buque, Iowa. In 1953, [he] joined the United Automobile
Workers International Union as a labor organizer.

[Watkins'] name had been mentioned by two witnesses who testified before the Committee at prior hearings. In September 1952, one Donald O. Spencer admitted having been a Communist from 1943 to 1946. He declared that he had been recruited into the Party with the endorsement and prior approval of [Watkins], whom he identified as the then District Vice-President of the Farm Equipment Workers. Spencer also mentioned that [Watkins] had attended meetings at which only card-carrying Communists were admitted. A month before [Watkins] testified, one Walter Rumsey stated that he had been recruited into the Party by [Watkins]. Rumsey added that he had paid Party dues to and later collected dues from [Watkins], who had assumed the name Sam Brown. Rumsey told the Committee that he left the Party in 1944.

[Watkins] answered these allegations freely and without reservation. His attitude toward the inquiry is clearly revealed from the statement he made when the questioning turned to the subject of his past conduct, associations and predilections:

"I am not now nor have I ever been a card-carrying member of the Communist Party.

"Rumsey was wrong when he said I had recruited him into the party, that I had received his dues, that I paid dues to him, and that I had used the alias Sam Brown.

"Spencer was wrong when he termed any meetings which I attended as closed Communist Party meetings.

"I would like to make it clear that for a period of time from approximately 1942 to 1947 I cooperated with the Communist Party and participated in Communist activities to such a degree that some persons may honestly believe that I was a member of the party.

"I have made contributions upon occasions to Communist causes. I have signed petitions for Communist causes. I attended caucuses at an FE convention at which Communist Party officials were present.

"Since I freely cooperated with the Communist Party I have no motive for making the distinction between co-operation and membership except the simple fact that it is the truth. I never carried a Communist Party card. I never accepted discipline and indeed on several occasions I opposed their position.

"In a special convention held in the summer of 1947 I led the fight for compliance with the Taft-Hartley Act by the FE-CIO International Union. This fight became so bitter that it ended any possibility of future cooperation."

The character of [Watkins'] testimony on these matters can perhaps best be summarized by the Government's own appraisal in its brief [written statement to the Court]:

"A more complete and candid statement of his past political associations and activities (treating the Communist Party for present purposes as a mere political party) can hardly be imagined. [Watkins] certainly was not attempting to conceal or withhold from the Committee his own past political associations, predilections, and preferences. Furthermore, [Watkins] told the Committee that he was entirely willing to identify for the Committee, and answer any questions it might have concerning, 'those persons whom I knew to be members of the Communist Party,' provided that, 'to [his] best knowledge and belief,' they still were members of the Party. . . ."

The Subcommittee, too, was apparently satisfied with [Watkins'] disclosures. After some further discussion elaborating on the statement, counsel for the Committee turned to another aspect of Rumsey's testimony. Rumsey had identified a group of persons whom he had known as members of the Communist Party, and counsel began to read this list of names to [Watkins]. [Watkins] stated that he did not know several of the persons. Of those whom he did know, he refused to tell whether he knew them to have been members of the Communist Party. He explained to the Subcommittee why he took such a position:

"I am not going to plead the Fifth Amendment, but I refuse to answer certain questions that I believe are outside the proper scope of your committee's activities. I will answer any questions which this committee puts to me about myself. I will also answer questions about those persons whom I knew to be members of the Communist Party and whom I believe still are. I will not, however, answer any questions with respect to others with whom I associated in the past. I do not believe that any law in this country requires me to testify about persons who may in the past have been Communist Party members or otherwise engaged in Communist Party activity but who to my best knowledge and belief have long since removed themselves from the Communist movement.

"I do not believe that such questions are relevant to the work of this committee nor do I believe that this committee has the right to undertake the public exposure of persons because of their past activities. I may be wrong, and the committee may have this power, but until and unless a court of law so holds and directs me to answer, I most firmly refuse to discuss the political activities of my past associates."

The Chairman of the Committee submitted a report of [Watkins'] refusal to answer questions to the House of Representatives. The House directed the Speaker to certify the Committee's report to the United States Attorney for initiation of criminal prosecution. A seven-count indictment [charge] was returned. [Watkins] waived his right to jury trial and was found guilty on all counts by the court. The sentence, a fine of $100 and one year in prison, was suspended, and [Watkins] was placed on probation.

An appeal was taken to the Court of Appeals for the District of Columbia. The conviction was reversed by a three-judge panel, one member dissenting. Upon rehearing en banc [with the participation of the entire court], the full bench affirmed [let stand] the conviction with the judges of the original majority in dissent. We granted certiorari [agreed to hear the case] because of the very important questions of constitutional law presented.

We start with several basic premises on which there is general agreement. The power of the Congress to conduct investigations is inherent in the legislative process. That power is broad. It encompasses inquiries concerning the administration of existing laws as well as proposed or possibly needed statutes. It includes surveys of defects in our social, economic or political system for the purpose of enabling the Congress to remedy them. It comprehends probes into departments of the Federal Government to expose corruption, inefficiency or waste. But broad as is this power of inquiry, it is not unlimited. There is no general authority to expose the private affairs of individuals without justification in terms of the functions of the Congress. This was freely conceded by the Solicitor General in his argument of this case. Nor is the Congress a law enforcement or trial agency. These are functions of the executive and judicial departments of government. No inquiry is an end in itself; it must be related to and in furtherance of a legitimate task of the

Congress. Investigations conducted solely for the personal aggrandizement of the investigators or to "punish" those investigated are indefensible.

It is unquestionably the duty of all citizens to cooperate with the Congress in its efforts to obtain the facts needed for intelligent legislative action. It is their unremitting obligation to respond to subpoenas, to respect the dignity of the Congress and its committees and to testify fully with respect to matters within the province of proper investigation. This, of course, assumes that the constitutional rights of witnesses will be respected by the Congress as they are in a court of justice.

The Bill of Rights is applicable to investigations as to all forms of governmental action. Witnesses cannot be compelled to give evidence against themselves. They cannot be subjected to unreasonable search and seizure. Nor can the First Amendment freedoms of speech, press, religion, or political belief and association be abridged.

The rudiments of the power to punish for "contempt of Congress" come to us from the pages of English history. The origin of privileges and contempts extends back into the period of the emergence of Parliament. The establishment of a legislative body which could challenge the absolute power of the monarch is a long and bitter story. In that struggle, Parliament made broad and varied use of the contempt power. Almost from the beginning, both the House of Commons and the House of Lords claimed absolute and plenary [complete] authority over their privileges. This was an independent body of law, described by Coke as lex parliamenti [the law of Parliament]. Only Parliament could declare what those privileges were or what new privileges were occasioned, and only Parliament could judge what conduct constituted a breach of privilege.

In particular, this exclusion of lex parliamenti from the lex terrae, or law of the land, precluded judicial review of the exercise of the contempt power or the assertion of privilege. Parliament declared that no court had jurisdiction [legal right] to consider such questions. In the latter part of the seventeenth century, an action [suit] for false imprisonment was brought by one Jay who had been held in contempt. The defendant, the Sergeant-at-Arms of the House of Commons, demurred [alleged] that he had taken the plaintiff [Jay] into custody for breach of privilege. The Chief Justice, Pemberton, overruled the demurrer. Summoned to the bar of the House, the Chief Justice explained that he believed that the assertion of privilege went to the merits [legal rights of the parties] of the action and did not preclude jurisdiction. For his audacity, the Chief Justice was dispatched to Newgate Prison.

It seems inevitable that the power claimed by Parliament would have been abused. Unquestionably it was. A few examples illustrate the way in which individual rights were infringed. During the seventeenth century, there was a violent upheaval, both religious and political. This was the time of the Reformation and the establishment of the Church of England. It was also the period when the Stuarts proclaimed that the royal prerogative was absolute. Ultimately there were two revolutions, one protracted and bloody, the second without bloodshed. Critical commentary of all kinds was treated as contempt of Parliament in these troubled days. Even clergymen were imprisoned for remarks made in their sermons. Perhaps the outstanding case arose from the private conversation of one Floyd, a Catholic, in which he expressed pleasure over the misfortune of the King's Protestant son-in-law and his wife. Floyd was not a member of Parliament. None of the persons concerned was in any way connected with the House of Commons. Nevertheless, that body imposed an humiliating and cruel sentence upon Floyd for contempt. The House of Lords intervened, rebuking the Commons for their extension of the privilege. The Commons acceded and transferred the record of the case to the Lords, who imposed substantially the same penalty.

Later in that century, during the reign of Charles II, there was great unrest over the fact that the heir apparent, James, had embraced Catholicism. Anti-Catholic feeling ran high, spilling over a few years later when the infamous rogue, Titus Oates, inflamed the country with rumors of a "Popish Plot" to murder the King. A committee of Parliament was appointed to learn the sources of certain pamphlets that had been appearing. One was entitled: *The Grand Question Concerning the Prorogation of this Parliament for a Year and Three Months Stated and Discussed.* A Doctor Carey admitted to the committee that he knew the author, but refused to divulge his name. Brought to the bar of the House of Lords, he persisted in this stand. The House imposed a fine of £1,000 and committed the witness to the Tower.

A hundred years later, George III had managed to gain control of Parliament through his ministers. The King could not silence the opposition, however, and one of the most vocal was John Wilkes. This precipitated a struggle that lasted for several years until Wilkes finally prevailed. One writer sums up the case thus:

"He had won a victory for freedom of the press. He had directed popular attention to the royally-controlled House of Commons, and pointed out its unrepresentative character, and had shown how easily a claim of privilege might be used to sanction the arbitrary proceedings of ministers and Parliament, even when a fundamental right of the subject was concerned. It is one of life's little ironies that work of such magnitude had been reserved for one of the worst libertines and demagogues of all time."

Even as late as 1835, the House of Commons appointed a select committee to inquire into ". . . the origin, nature, extent and tendency of the Orange Institutions." This was a political-religious organization, vehemently Protestant in religion and strongly in favor of the growth of the British Empire. The committee summoned the Deputy Grand Secretary and demanded that he produce all the records of the organization. The witness refused to turn over a letter-book, which he admitted contained his answers to many communications upon Orange business. But it also contained, he said, records of private communications with respect to Orangeism. Summoned to the bar of the House of Commons, he remained adamant and was committed to Newgate Prison.

Modern times have seen a remarkable restraint in the use by Parliament of its contempt power. Important investigations, like those conducted in America by congressional committees, are made by Royal Commissions of inquiry. These commissions are comprised of experts in the problem to be studied. They are removed from the turbulent forces of politics and partisan considerations. Seldom, if ever, have these commissions been given the authority to compel the testimony of witnesses or the production of documents. Their success in fulfilling their fact-finding missions without resort to coercive tactics is a tribute to the fairness of the processes to the witnesses and their close adherence to the subject matter committed to them.

The history of contempt of the legislature in this country is notably different from that of England. In the early days of the United States, there lingered the direct knowledge of the evil effects of absolute power. Most of the instances of use of compulsory process by the first Congresses concerned matters affecting the qualification or integrity of their members or came about in inquiries dealing with suspected corruption or mismanagement of government officials. Unlike the English practice, from the very outset the use of contempt power by the legislature was deemed subject to judicial review.

There was very little use of the power of compulsory process in early years to enable the Congress to obtain facts pertinent to the enactment of new statutes or the administration of existing laws. The first occasion for such an investigation arose in 1827 when the House of Representatives was considering a revision of the tariff laws. In the Senate, there was no use of a fact-finding investigation in aid of legislation until 1859. In the Legislative Reorganization Act, the Committee on Un-American Activities was the only standing committee of the House of Representatives that was given the power to compel disclosures.

It is not surprising, from the fact that the Houses of Congress so sparingly employed the power to conduct investigations, that there have been few cases requiring judicial review of the power. The nation was almost one hundred years old before the first case reached this Court to challenge the use of compulsory process as a legislative device, rather than in inquiries concerning the elections or privileges of Congressmen. In *Kilbourn v. Thompson*, decided in 1881, an investigation had been authorized by the House of Representatives to learn the circumstances surrounding the bankruptcy of Jay Cooke & Company, in which the United States had deposited funds. The committee became particularly interested in a private real estate pool that was a part of the financial structure. The Court found that the subject matter of the inquiry was "in its nature clearly judicial and therefore one in respect to which no valid legislation could be enacted." The House had thereby exceeded the limits of its own authority.

Subsequent to the decision in *Kilbourn*, until recent times, there were very few cases dealing with the investigative power. The matter came to the fore again when the Senate undertook to study the corruption in the handling of oil leases in the 1920's. In *McGrain v. Daugherty* and *Sinclair v. U.S.*, the Court applied the precepts of *Kilbourn* to uphold the authority of the Congress to conduct the challenged investigations. The Court recognized the danger to effective and honest conduct of the Government if the legislature's power to probe corruption in the executive branch were unduly hampered.

Following these important decisions, there was another lull in judicial review of investigations. The absence of challenge, however, was not indicative of the absence of inquiries. To the contrary, there was vigorous use of the investigative process by a Congress bent upon harnessing and directing the vast economic and social forces of the times. Only one case came before this Court, and the authority of the Congress was affirmed.

In the decade following World War II, there appeared a new kind of congressional inquiry unknown in prior periods of American history. Principally this was the result of the various investigations into the threat of subversion of the United States Government, but other subjects of congressional interest also contributed to the changed scene. This new phase of legislative inquiry involved a broad-scale intrusion into the lives and affairs of private citizens. It brought before the courts novel questions of the appropriate limits of congressional inquiry. Prior cases, like *Kilbourn*, *McGrain* and *Sinclair*, had defined the scope of investigative power in terms of the inherent limitations of the sources of that power. In the more recent cases, the emphasis shifted to problems of accommodating the interest of the Government with the rights and privileges of individuals. The central theme was the application of the Bill of Rights as a restraint upon the assertion of governmental power in this form.

It was during this period that the Fifth Amendment privilege against self-incrimination was frequently invoked and recognized as a legal limit upon the authority of a committee to require that a witness answer its questions. Some early doubts as to the applicability of that privilege before a legislative committee never matured. When the matter reached this Court, the Government did not challenge in any way that the Fifth Amendment protection was available to the witness, and such a challenge could not have prevailed. It confined its argument to the character of the answers sought and to the adequacy of the claim of privilege.

A far more difficult task evolved from the claim by witnesses that the committees' interrogations were infringements upon the freedoms of the First Amendment. Clearly, an investigation is subject to the command that the Congress shall make no law abridging freedom of speech or press or assembly. While it is true that there is no statute to be reviewed, and that an investigation is not a law, nevertheless an investigation is part of law-making. It is justified solely as an adjunct to the legislative process. The First Amendment may be invoked against infringement of the protected freedoms by law or by law-making.

Abuses of the investigative process may imperceptibly lead to abridgment of protected freedoms. The mere summoning of a witness and compelling him to testify, against his will, about his beliefs, expressions or associations is a measure of governmental interference. And when those forced revelations concern matters that are unorthodox, unpopular, or even hateful to the general public, the reaction in the life of the witness may be disastrous. This effect is even more harsh when it is past beliefs, expressions or associations that are disclosed and judged by current standards rather than those contemporary with the matters exposed.

Nor does the witness alone suffer the consequences. Those who are identified by witnesses and thereby placed in the same glare of publicity are equally subject to public stigma, scorn and obloquy. Beyond that, there is the more subtle and immeasurable effect upon those who tend to adhere to the most orthodox and uncontroversial views and associations in order to avoid a similar fate at some future time. That this impact is partly the result of non-governmental activity by private persons cannot relieve the investigators of their responsibility for initiating the reaction.

The Court recognized the restraints of the Bill of Rights upon congressional investigations in *U.S. v. Rumely*. The magnitude and complexity of the problem of applying the First Amendment to that case led the Court to construe [interpret] narrowly the resolution describing the committee's authority. It was concluded that, when First Amendment rights are threatened, the delegation of power to the committee must be clearly revealed in its charter.

Accommodation of the congressional need for particular information with the individual and personal interest in privacy is an arduous and delicate task for any court. We do not underestimate the difficulties that would attend such an undertaking. It is manifest that despite the adverse effects which follow upon compelled disclosure of private matters, not all such inquiries are barred. *Kilbourn* teaches that such an investigation into individual affairs is invalid if unrelated to any legislative purpose. That is beyond the powers conferred upon the Congress in the Constitution. *Rumely* makes it plain that the mere semblance of legislative purpose would not justify an inquiry in the face of the Bill of Rights. The critical element is the existence of, and the weight to be ascribed to, the interest of the Congress in demanding disclosures from an unwilling witness. We cannot simply assume, however, that every congressional investigation is justified by a public need that over-balances any private rights affected. To do so would be to abdicate the responsibility placed by the Constitution upon the judiciary to insure that the Congress does not unjustifiably encroach upon an individual's right to privacy nor abridge his liberty of speech, press, religion or assembly.

[Watkins] has earnestly suggested that the difficult questions of protecting these rights from infringement by legislative inquiries can be surmounted in this case because there was no public purpose served in his interrogation. His conclusion is based upon the thesis that the Subcommittee was engaged in a program of exposure for the sake of exposure. The sole purpose of the inquiry, he contends, was to bring down upon himself and others the violence of public reaction because of their past beliefs, expressions and associations. In support of this argument, [Watkins] has marshalled an impressive array of evidence that some Congressmen have believed that such was their duty, or part of it.

We have no doubt that there is no congressional power to expose for the sake of exposure. The public is, of course, entitled to be informed concerning the workings of its government. That cannot be inflated into a general power to expose where the predominant result can only be an invasion of the private rights of individuals. But a solution to our problem is not to be found in testing the motives of committee members for this purpose. Such is not our function. Their motives alone would not vitiate an investigation which had been instituted by a House of Congress if that assembly's legislative purpose is being served.

[Watkins'] contentions do point to a situation of particular significance from the standpoint of the constitutional limitations upon congressional investigations. The theory of a committee inquiry is that the committee members are serving as the representatives of the parent assembly in collecting information for a legislative purpose. Their function is to act as the eyes and ears of the Congress in obtaining facts upon which the full legislature can act. To carry out this mission, committees and subcommittees, sometimes one Congressman, are endowed with the full power of the Congress to compel testimony. In this case, only two men exercised that authority in demanding information over [Watkins'] protest.

An essential premise in this situation is that the House or Senate shall have instructed the committee members on what they are to do with the power delegated to them. It is the responsibility of the Congress, in the first instance, to insure that compulsory process is used only in furtherance of a legislative purpose. That requires that the instructions to an investigating committee spell out that group's jurisdiction and purpose with sufficient particularity. Those instructions are embodied in the authorizing resolution. That document is the committee's charter. Broadly drafted and loosely worded, however, such resolutions can leave tremendous latitude to the discretion of the investigators. The more vague the committee's charter is, the greater becomes the possibility that the committee's specific actions are not in conformity with the will of the parent House of Congress.

The authorizing resolution of the Un-American Activities Committee was adopted in 1938 when a select committee, under the chairmanship of Representative Dies, was created. Several years later, the Committee was made a standing organ of the House with the same mandate. It defines the Committee's authority as follows:

"The Committee on Un-American Activities, as a whole or by subcommittee, is authorized to make from time to time investigations of

(i) the extent, character, and objects of un-American propaganda activities in the United States,

(ii) the diffusion within the United States of subversive and un-American propaganda that is instigated from foreign countries or of a domestic origin and attacks the principle of the form of government as guaranteed by our Constitution, and

(iii) all other questions in relation thereto that would aid Congress in any necessary remedial legislation."

It would be difficult to imagine a less explicit authorizing resolution. Who can define the meaning of "un--American"? What is that single, solitary "principle of the form of government as guaranteed by our Constitution"? There is no need to dwell upon the language, however. At one time, perhaps, the resolution might have been read narrowly to confine the Committee to the subject of propaganda. The events that have transpired in the fifteen years before the interrogation of [Watkins] make such a construction impossible at this date.

The members of the Committee have clearly demonstrated that they did not feel themselves restricted in any way to propaganda in the narrow sense of the word. Unquestionably the Committee conceived of its task in the grand view of its name. Un-American activities were its target, no matter how or where manifested. Notwithstanding the broad purview of the Committee's experience, the House of Representatives repeatedly approved its continuation. Five times it extended the life of the special committee. Then it made the group a standing committee of the House. A year later, the Committee's charter was embodied in the Legislative Reorganization Act. On five occasions, at the beginning of sessions of Congress, it has made the authorizing resolution part of the rules of the House. On innumerable occasions, it has passed appropriation bills to allow the Committee to continue its efforts.

Combining the language of the resolution with the construction it has been given, it is evident that the preliminary control of the Committee exercised by the House of Representatives is slight or non-existent. No one could reasonably deduce from the charter the kind of investigation that the Committee was directed to make. As a result, we are asked to engage in a process of retroactive rationalization. Looking backward from the events that transpired, we are asked to uphold the Committee's actions unless it appears that they were clearly not authorized by the charter. As a corollary to this inverse approach, the Government urges that we must view the matter hospitably to the power of the Congress - that if there is any legislative purpose which might have been furthered by the kind of disclosure sought, the witness must be punished for withholding it. No doubt every reasonable indulgence of legality must be accorded to the actions of a coordinate branch of our Government. But such deference cannot yield to an unnecessary and unreasonable dissipation of precious constitutional freedoms.

The Government contends that the public interest at the core of the investigations of the Un-American Activities Committee is the need by the Congress to be informed of efforts to overthrow the Government by force and violence so that adequate legislative safeguards can be erected. From this core, however, the Committee can radiate outward infinitely to any topic thought to be related in some way to armed insurrection. The outer reaches of this domain are known only by the content of "un-American activities." Remoteness of subject can be aggravated by a probe for a depth of detail even farther removed from any basis of legislative action. A third dimension is added when the investigators turn their attention to the past to collect minutiae on remote topics, on the hypothesis that the past may reflect upon the present.

The consequences that flow from this situation are manifold. In the first place, a reviewing court is unable to make the kind of judgment made by the Court in *Rumely*. The Committee is allowed, in essence, to define its own authority, to choose the direction and focus of its activities. In deciding what to do with the power that has been conferred upon them, members of the Committee may act pursuant to motives that seem to them to be the highest. Their decisions, nevertheless, can lead to ruthless exposure of private lives in order to gather data that is neither desired by the Congress nor useful to it. Yet it is impossible in this circumstance, with constitutional freedoms in jeopardy, to declare that the Committee has ranged beyond the area committed to it by its parent assembly because the boundaries are so nebulous.

More important and more fundamental than that, however, it insulates the House that has authorized the investigation from the witnesses who are subjected to the sanctions of compulsory process. There is a wide gulf between the responsibility for the use of investigative power and the actual exercise of that power. This is an especially vital consideration in assuring respect for constitutional liberties. Protected freedoms should not be placed in danger in the absence of a clear determination by the House or the Senate that a particular inquiry is justified by a specific legislative need.

It is, of course, not the function of this Court to prescribe rigid rules for the Congress to follow in drafting resolutions establishing investigating committees. That is a matter peculiarly within the realm of the legislature, and its decisions will be accepted by the courts up to the point where their own duty to enforce the constitutionally protected rights of individuals is affected.

An excessively broad charter, like that of the House Un-American Activities Committee, places the courts in an untenable position if they are to strike a balance between the public need for a particular interrogation and the right of citizens to carry on their affairs free from unnecessary governmental interference. It is impossible in such a situation to ascertain whether any legislative purpose justifies the disclosures sought and, if so, the importance of that information to the Congress in furtherance of its legislative function. The reason no court can make this critical judgment is that the House of Representatives itself has never made it. Only the legislative assembly initiating an investigation can assay the relative necessity of specific disclosures.

Absence of the qualitative consideration of [Watkins'] questioning by the House of Representatives aggravates a serious problem, revealed in this case, in the relationship of congressional investigating committees and the witnesses who appear before them. Plainly these committees are restricted to the missions delegated to them, i.e., to acquire certain data to be used by the House or the Senate in coping with a problem that falls within its legislative sphere. No witness can be compelled to make disclosures on matters outside that area. . . .

Since World War II, the Congress has practically abandoned its original practice of utilizing the coercive sanction of contempt proceedings at the bar of the House. The sanction there imposed is imprisonment by the House until the recalcitrant witness agrees to testify or disclose the matters sought, provided that the incarceration does not extend beyond adjournment. The Congress has instead invoked the aid of the federal judicial system in protecting itself against contumacious conduct. It has become customary to refer these matters to the United States Attorneys for prosecution under criminal law.

The appropriate statute is found in [the United States Code]. It provides:

> "Every person who having been summoned as a witness by the authority of either House of Congress to give testimony or to produce papers upon any matter under inquiry before either House, or any joint committee established by a joint or concurrent resolution of the two Houses of Congress, or any committee of either House of Congress, willfully makes default, or who, having appeared, refuses to answer any question pertinent to the question under inquiry, shall be deemed guilty of a misdemeanor, punishable by a fine of not more than $1,000 nor less than $100 and imprisonment in a common jail for not less than one month nor more than twelve months."

In fulfillment of their obligation under this statute, the courts must accord to the defendants [parties charged with an act] every right which is guaranteed to defendants in all other criminal cases. Among these is the right to have available, through a sufficiently precise statute, information revealing the standard of criminality before the commission of the alleged offense. Applied to persons prosecuted under [this section], this raises a special problem in that the statute defines the crime as refusal to answer "any question pertinent to the question under inquiry." Part of the standard of criminality, therefore, is the pertinency of the questions propounded to the witness.

The problem attains proportion when viewed from the standpoint of the witness who appears before a congressional committee. He must decide at the time the questions are propounded whether or not to answer. As the Court said in *Sinclair*, the witness acts at his peril. He is ". . . bound rightly to construe the statute." An erroneous determination on his part, even if made in the utmost good faith, does not exculpate [excuse] him if the court should later rule that the questions were pertinent to the question under inquiry.

It is obvious that a person compelled to make this choice is entitled to have knowledge of the subject to which the interrogation is deemed pertinent. That knowledge must be available with the same degree of explicitness and clarity that the Due Process Clause requires in the expression of any element of a criminal offense. The "vice of vagueness" must be avoided here as in all other crimes. There are several sources that can outline the "question under inquiry" in such a way that the rules against vagueness are satisfied. The authorizing resolution, the remarks of the chairman or members of the committee, or even the nature of the proceedings themselves might sometimes make the topic clear. This case demonstrates, however, that these sources often leave the matter in grave doubt.

The first possibility is that the authorizing resolution itself will so clearly declare the "question under inquiry" that a witness can understand the pertinency of questions asked him. The Government does not contend that the authorizing resolution of the Un-American Activities Committee could serve such a purpose. Its confusing breadth is amply illustrated by the innumerable and diverse questions into which the Committee has inquired under this charter since 1938. If the "question under inquiry" were stated with such sweeping and uncertain scope, we doubt that it would withstand an attack on the ground of vagueness.

That issue is not before us, however, in light of the Government's position that the immediate subject under inquiry before the Subcommittee interviewing [Watkins] was only one aspect of the Committee's authority to investigate un-American activities. Distilling that single topic from the broad field is an extremely difficult task. . . . There was an opening statement by the Committee Chairman at the outset of the hearing, but this gives us no guidance. In this statement, the Chairman did no more than paraphrase the authorizing resolution and give a very general sketch of the past efforts of the Committee.

No aid is given as to the "question under inquiry" in the action of the full Committee that authorized the creation of the Subcommittee before which [Watkins] appeared. The Committee adopted a formal resolution giving the Chairman the power to appoint subcommittees ". . . for the purpose of performing any and all acts which the Committee as a whole is authorized to do." In effect, this was a device to enable the investigations to proceed with a quorum of one or two members and sheds no light on the relevancy of the questions asked of [Watkins].

The Government believes that the topic of inquiry before the Subcommittee concerned Communist infiltration in labor. In his introductory remarks, the Chairman made reference to a bill, then pending before the Committee, which would have penalized labor unions controlled or dominated by persons who were, or had been, members of a "Communist-action" organization, as defined in the Internal Security Act of 1950. The Subcommittee, it is contended, might have been endeavoring to determine the extent of such a problem.

This view is corroborated somewhat by the witnesses who preceded and followed [Watkins] before the Subcommittee. Looking at the entire hearings, however, there is strong reason to doubt that the subject revolved about labor matters. The published transcript is entitled: *Investigation of Communist*

Activities in the Chicago Area, and six of the nine witnesses had no connection with labor at all.

The most serious doubts as to the Subcommittee's "question under inquiry," however, stem from the precise questions that [Watkins] has been charged with refusing to answer. Under the terms of the statute, after all, it is these which must be proved pertinent. [Watkins] is charged with refusing to tell the Subcommittee whether or not he knew that certain named persons had been members of the Communist Party in the past. The Subcommittee's counsel read the list from the testimony of a previous witness who had identified them as Communists. Although this former witness was identified with labor, he had not stated that the persons he named were involved in union affairs. Of the thirty names propounded to [Watkins], seven were completely unconnected with organized labor. One operated a beauty parlor. Another was a watchmaker. Several were identified as "just citizens" or "only Communists." When almost a quarter of the persons on the list are not labor people, the inference becomes strong that the subject before the Subcommittee was not defined in terms of Communism in labor.

The final source of evidence as to the "question under inquiry" is the Chairman's response when [Watkins] objected to the questions on the grounds of lack of pertinency. The Chairman then announced that the Subcommittee was investigating "subversion and subversive propaganda." This is a subject at least as broad and indefinite as the authorizing resolution of the Committee, if not more so.

Having exhausted the several possible indicia of the "question under inquiry," we remain unenlightened as to the subject to which the questions asked [Watkins] were pertinent. Certainly, if the point is that obscure after trial and appeal, it was not adequately revealed to [Watkins] when he had to decide at his peril whether or not to answer. Fundamental fairness demands that no witness be compelled to make such a determination with so little guidance. Unless the subject matter has been made to appear with undisputable clarity, it is the duty of the investigative body, upon objection of the witness on grounds of pertinency, to state for the record the subject under inquiry at that time and the manner in which the propounded questions are pertinent thereto. To be meaningful, the explanation must describe what the topic under inquiry is and the connective reasoning whereby the precise questions asked relate to it.

The statement of the Committee Chairman in this case, in response to [Watkins'] protest, was woefully inadequate to convey sufficient information as to the pertinency of the questions to the subject under inquiry. [Watkins] was thus not accorded a fair opportunity to determine whether he was within his rights in refusing to answer, and his conviction is necessarily invalid under the Due Process Clause of the Fifth Amendment.

We are mindful of the complexities of modern government and the ample scope that must be left to the Congress as the sole constitutional depository of legislative power. Equally mindful are we of the indispensable function, in the exercise of that power, of congressional investigations. The conclusions we have reached in this case will not prevent the Congress, through its committees, from obtaining any information it needs for the proper fulfillment of its role in our scheme of government. The legislature is free to determine the kinds of data that should be collected. It is only those investigations that are conducted by use of compulsory process that give rise to a need to protect the rights of individuals against illegal encroachment. That protection can be readily achieved through procedures which prevent the separation of power from responsibility and which provide the constitutional requisites of fairness for witnesses. A measure of added care on the part of the House and the Senate in authorizing the use of compulsory process and by their committees in exercising that power would suffice. That is a small price to pay if it serves to uphold the principles of limited, constitutional government without constricting the power of the Congress to inform itself.

The judgment of the Court of Appeals is reversed, and the case is remanded [returned] to the District Court with instructions to dismiss the indictment.

Justice Tom Clark, dissenting: As I see it, the chief fault in the majority opinion is its mischievous curbing of the informing function of the Congress. While I am not versed in its procedures, my experience in the executive branch of the Government leads me to believe that the requirements laid down in the opinion for the operation of the committee system of inquiry are both unnecessary and unworkable. It is my purpose to first discuss this phase of the opinion and then record my views on the merits of Watkins' case.

It may be that at times the House Committee on Un-American Activities has, as the Court says, "conceived of its task in the grand view of its name." And, perhaps, as the Court indicates, the rules of conduct placed upon the Committee by the House admit of individual abuse and unfairness. But that is none of our affair. So long as the object of a legislative inquiry is legitimate and the questions propounded are pertinent thereto, it is not for the courts to interfere with the committee system of inquiry. To hold otherwise would be an infringement on the power given the Congress to inform itself, and thus a trespass upon the fundamental American principle of separation of powers. The majority has substituted the judiciary as the grand inquisitor and supervisor of congressional investigations. It has never been so.

Legislative committees to inquire into facts or conditions for assurance of the public welfare or to determine the need for legislative action have grown in importance with the complexity of government. The investigation that gave rise to this prosecution is of the latter type. Since many matters requiring statutory action lie in the domain of the specialist or are unknown without testimony from informed witnesses, the need for information has brought about legislative inquiries that have used the compulsion of the subpoena [order to give testimony] to lay bare needed facts and a statute . . . here involved, to punish recalcitrant witnesses. The propriety of investigations has long been recognized and rarely curbed by the courts, though constitutional limitations on the investigatory powers are admitted. The use of legislative committees to secure information follows the example of the people from whom our legislative system is derived. The British method has variations from that of the United States but fundamentally serves the same purpose - the enlightenment of Parliament for the better performance of its duties. There are standing committees to carry on the routine work, royal commissions to grapple with important social or economic problems, and special tribunals of inquiry for some alleged offense in government. Our Congress has since its beginning used the committee system to inform itself. It has been estimated that over 600 investigations have been conducted since the First Congress. They are "a necessary and appropriate attribute of the power to legislate. . . ."

The Court indicates that in this case the source of the trouble lies in the "tremendous latitude" given the Un-American Activities Committee in the Legislative Reorganization Act. It finds that the Committee "is allowed, in essence, to define its own authority, [and] to choose the direction and focus of its activities." This, of course, is largely true of all committees within their respective spheres. And, while it is necessary that the "charter," as the opinion calls the enabling resolution, "spell out [its] jurisdiction and purpose," that must necessarily be in more or less general terms. An examination of the enabling resolutions of other committees reveals the extent to which this is true.

Permanent or standing committees of both Houses have been given power in exceedingly broad terms. For example, the Committees on the Armed Services have jurisdiction over "Common defense generally"; the Committees on Interstate and Foreign Commerce have jurisdiction over "Interstate and foreign commerce generally"; and the Committees on Appropriation have jurisdiction over "Appropriation of the revenue for the support of the Government." Perhaps even more important for purposes of comparison are the broad authorizations given to select or special committees established by the Congress from time to time. Such committees have been "authorized and directed" to make full and complete studies "of whether organized crime utilizes the facilities of interstate commerce or otherwise operates in interstate commerce"; "of . . . all lobbying activities intended to influence, encourage, promote, or retard legislation"; "to determine the extent to which current literature . . . containing immoral, [or] obscene . . . matter, or placing improper emphasis on crime . . . are being made available to the people of the United States . . ."; and "of the extent to which criminal or other improper practices . . . are, or have been, engaged in the field of labor-management relations . . . to the detriment of the interests of the public. . . ." Surely these authorizations permit the committees even more "tremendous latitude" than the "charter" of the Un-American Activities Committee. Yet no one has suggested that the powers granted were too broad. To restrain and limit the . . . investigative power of this Committee necessitates the similar handling of all other committees. The resulting restraint imposed on the committee system appears to cripple the system beyond workability.

The Court finds fault with the use made of compulsory process, power for the use of which is granted the Committee in the Reorganization Act. While the Court finds that the Congress is free "to determine the kinds of data" it wishes its committees to collect, this has lead, the Court says, to an encroachment on individual rights through the abuse of process. To my mind this indicates a lack of understanding of the problems facing such committees. I am sure that the committees would welcome voluntary disclosure. It would simplify and relieve their burden considerably if the parties involved in investigations would come forward with a frank willingness to cooperate. But everyday experience shows this just does not happen. One needs only to read the newspapers to know that the Congress could gather little "data" unless its committees had, unfettered, the power of subpoena. In fact, Watkins himself could not be found for appearance at the first hearing and it was only by subpoena that he attended the second. The Court generalizes on this crucial problem saying "added care on the part of the House and the Senate in authorizing the use of compulsory process and by their committees in exercising that power would suffice." It does not say how this "added care" could be applied in practice; however, there are many implications since the opinion warns that "procedures which prevent the separation of power from responsibility" would be necessary along with "constitutional requisites of fairness for witnesses." The "power" and "responsibility" for the investigations are, of course, in the House where the proceeding is initiated. But the investigating job itself can only be done through the use of committees. They must have the "power" to force compliance with their requirements. If the rule requires that this power be retained in the full House then investigations will be so cumbrous that their conduct will be a practical impossibility. As to "fairness for witnesses" there is nothing in the record showing any abuse of Watkins. If anything, the Committee was abused by his recalcitrance.

While ambiguity prevents exactness (and there is "vice in vagueness" the majority reminds), the sweep of the opinion seems to be that "preliminary control" of the Committee must be exercised. The Court says a witness' protected freedoms cannot "be placed in danger in the absence of a clear determination by the House or the Senate that a particular inquiry is justified by a specific legislative need." Frankly I do not see how any such procedure as "preliminary control" can be effected in either House of the Congress. What will be controlled preliminarily? The plans of the investigation, the necessity of calling certain witnesses, the questions to be asked, the details of subpoenas . . . , etc.? As it is now, Congress is hard pressed to find sufficient time to fully debate and adopt all needed legislation. The Court asserts that "the Congress has practically abandoned its original practice of utilizing the coercive sanction of contempt proceedings at the bar of the House." This was to be expected. It may be that back in the twenties and thirties Congress could spare the time to conduct contempt hearings, but that appears impossible now. The Court places a greater burden in the conduct of contempt cases before the courts than it does before "the bar of the House." It cites with approval cases of contempt tried before a House of the Congress where no more safeguards were present than we find here. In contempt prosecutions before a court, however, the majority places an investigative hearing on a par with a criminal trial, requiring that "knowledge of the subject to which the interrogation is deemed pertinent . . . must be available [to the witness] with the same degree of explicitness and clarity that the Due Process Clause requires in the expression of any element of a criminal offense." I know of no such claim ever being made before.

Such a requirement has never been thought applicable to investigations and is wholly out of place when related to the informing function of the Congress. The Congress does not have the facts at the time of the investigation for it is the facts that are being sought. In a criminal trial the investigation has been completed and all of the facts are at hand. The informing function of the Congress is in effect "a study by the government of circumstances which seem to call for study in the public interest." In the conduct of such a proceeding it is impossible to be as explicit and exact as in a criminal prosecution. If the Court is saying that its new rule does not apply to contempt cases tried before the bar of the House affected, it may well lead to trial of all contempt cases before the bar of the whole House in order to avoid the restrictions of the rule. But this will not promote the result desired by the majority. Summary treatment, at best, could be provided before the whole House because of the time factor, and such treatment would necessarily deprive the witness of many of the safeguards in the present procedures. On review here the majority might then find fault with that procedure.

Coming to the merits of Watkins' case, the Court reverses the judgment because: (1) The subject matter of the inquiry was not "made to appear with undisputable clarity" either through its "charter" or by the Chairman at the time of the hearing and, therefore, Watkins was deprived of a clear understanding of "the manner in which the propounded questions [were] pertinent thereto"; and (2) the present committee system of inquiry of the House, as practiced by the Un-American Activities Committee, does not provide adequate safeguards for the protection of the constitutional right of free speech. I subscribe to neither conclusion.

Watkins had been an active leader in the labor movement for many years and had been identified by two previous witnesses at the Committee's hearing in Chicago as a member of the Communist Party. There can be no question that he was fully informed of the subject matter of the inquiry. His testimony reveals a complete knowledge and understanding of the hearings at Chicago. There the Chairman had announced that the Committee had been directed "to ascertain the extent and success of subversive activities directed against these United States [and] on the basis of these investigations and hearings . . . [report] its findings to the Congress and [make] recommendations . . . for new legislation." He pointed to the various laws that had been enacted as a result of Committee recommendations. He stated that "The Congress has also referred to the House Committee on Un-American Activities a bill which would amend the National Security Act of 1950" which, if made law, would restrict the availability of the Labor Act to unions not "in fact Communist-controlled action groups." The Chairman went on to say that, "It cannot be said that subversive infiltration has had a greater nor a lesser success in infiltrating this important area. The hearings today are the culmination of an investigation. . . . Every witness who has been subpoenaed to appear before the committee here in Chicago . . . [is] known to possess information which will assist the Committee in performing its directed function to the Congress of the United States."

A subpoena had issued for Watkins to appear at the Chicago hearings but he was not served. After Watkins was served, the hearing in question was held in Washington, D.C. Reference at this hearing was made to the one conducted in Chicago. Watkins came before the Committee with a carefully prepared statement. He denied certain testimony of the previous witnesses and declared that he had never been a "card carrying member" of the Party. He admitted that for the period 1942-1947 he "cooperated with the Communist Party . . . participated in Communist activities . . . made contributions . . . attended caucuses at [his union's] convention at which Communist Party officials were present [and] freely cooperated with the Communist Party. . . ." This indicated that for a five-year period he, a union official, was cooperating closely with the Communist Party, even permitting its officials to attend union caucuses. For the last two years of this liaison the Party had publicly thrown off its cloak of a political party. It was a reconstituted, militant group known to be dedicated to the overthrow of our Government by force and violence. In this setting the Committee attempted to have Watkins identify thirty persons, most of whom were connected with labor unions in some way. While one "operated a beauty parlor" and another was "a watchmaker," they may well have been "drops" or other functionaries in the program of cooperation between the union and the Party. It is a non sequitur for the Court to say that since "almost a quarter of the persons on the list are not labor people, the inference becomes strong that the subject before the Subcommittee was not defined in terms of Communism in labor." I submit that the opposite is true.

I think the Committee here was acting entirely within its scope and that the purpose of its inquiry was set out with "undisputable clarity." In the first place, the authorizing language of the Reorganization Act must be read as a whole, not dissected. It authorized investigation into subversive activity, its extent, character, objects, and diffusion. While the language might have been more explicit than using such words as "un-American," or phrases like "principle of the form of government," still these are fairly well understood terms. We must construe [interpret] them to give them meaning if we can. Our cases indicate that rather than finding fault with the use of words or phrases, we are bound to presume that the action of the legislative body in granting authority to the Committee was with a legitimate object "if [the action] is capable of being so construed." Before we can deny the authority "it must be obvious that" the Committee has "exceeded the bounds of legislative power." The fact that the Committee has often been attacked has caused close scrutiny of its acts by the House as a whole and the House has repeatedly given the Committee its approval. "Power" and "responsibility" have not been separated. But the record in this case does not stop here. It shows that at the hearings involving Watkins, the Chairman made statements explaining the functions of the committee. And, furthermore, Watkins' action at the hearing clearly reveals that he was well acquainted with the purpose of the hearing. It was to investigate Communist infiltration into his union. This certainly falls within the grant of authority from the Reorganization Act and the House has had ample opportunity to limit the investigative scope of the Committee if it feels that the Committee has exceeded its legitimate bounds.

The Court makes much of [Watkins'] claim of "exposure for exposure's sake" and strikes at the purposes of the Committee through this catch phrase. But we are bound to accept as the purpose of the Committee that stated in the Reorganization Act together with the statements of the Chairman at the hearings involved here. Nothing was said of exposure. The statements of a single Congressman cannot transform the real purpose of the Committee into something not authorized by the parent resolution. The Court indicates that the questions propounded were asked for exposure's sake and had no pertinency to the inquiry. It appears to me that they were entirely pertinent to the announced purpose of the Committee's inquiry. Undoubtedly Congress has the power to inquire into the subjects of Communism and the Communist Party. As a corollary of the congressional power to inquire into such subject matter, the Congress, through its committees, can legitimately seek to identify individual members of the Party.

The pertinency of the questions is highlighted by the need for the Congress to know the extent of infiltration of Communism in labor unions. This technique of infiltration was that used in bringing the downfall of countries formerly free but now still remaining behind the Iron Curtain. The Douds Case illustrates that the Party is not an ordinary political party and has not been at least since 1945. Association with its officials is not an ordinary association. Nor does it matter that the questions related to the past. Influences of past associations often linger on as was clearly shown in the instance of the witness Matusow and others. The techniques used in the infiltration which admittedly existed here might well be used again in the future. If the parties about whom Watkins was interrogated were Communists and collaborated with him, as a prior witness indicated, an entirely new area of investigation might have been opened up. Watkins' silence prevented the Committee from learning this information which could have been vital to its future investigation. The Committee was likewise entitled to elicit testimony showing the truth or falsity of the prior testimony of the witnesses who had involved Watkins and the union with collaboration with the Party. If the testimony was untrue a false picture of the relationship between the union and the Party leaders would have resulted. For these reasons there were ample indications of the pertinency of the questions.

The Court condemns the long-established and long-recognized committee system of inquiry of the House because it raises serious questions concerning the protection it affords to constitutional rights. It concludes that compelling a witness to reveal his "beliefs, expressions or associations" impinges upon First Amendment rights. The system of inquiry, it says, must "insure that the Congress does not unjustifiably encroach upon an individual's right to privacy nor abridge his liberty of speech, press, religion or assembly." In effect the Court honors Watkins' claim of a "right to silence" which brings all inquiries, as we know, to a "dead end." I do not see how any First Amendment rights were endangered here. There is nothing in the First Amendment that provides the guarantees Watkins claims. That Amendment was designed to prevent attempts by law to curtail freedom of speech. It forbids Congress from making any law "abridging the freedom of speech, or of the press." It guarantees Watkins' right to join any organization and make any speech that does not have an intent to incite to crime. But Watkins was asked whether he knew named individuals and whether they were Communists. He refused to answer on the ground that his rights were being abridged. What he was actually seeking to do was to protect his former associates, not himself, from embarrassment. He had already admitted his own involvement. He sought to vindicate the rights, if any, of his associates. It is settled that one cannot invoke the constitutional rights of another.

As already indicated, even if Watkins' associates were on the stand they could not decline to disclose their Communist connections on First Amendment grounds. While there may be no restraint by the Government of one's beliefs, the right of free belief has never been extended to include the withholding of knowledge of past events or transactions. There is no general privilege of silence. The First Amendment does not make speech or silence permissible to a person in such measure as he chooses. Watkins has here exercised his own choice as to when he talks, what questions he answers, and when he remains silent. A witness is not given such a choice by the Amendment. Remote and indirect disadvantages such as "public stigma, scorn and obloquy" may be related to the First Amendment, but they are not enough to block investigation. The Congress has recognized this since 1862 when it first adopted the contempt section.

We do not have in this case unauthorized, arbitrary, or unreasonable inquiries and disclosures with respect to a witness' personal and private affairs. . . . [This is not] "a new kind of congressional inquiry unknown in prior periods of American history . . . [i. e.] a broad scale intrusion into the lives and affairs of private citizens." As I see it only the setting is different. It involves new faces and new issues brought about by new situations which the Congress feels it is necessary to control in the public interest. The difficulties of getting information are identical if not greater. Like authority to that always used by the Congress is employed here and in the same manner so far as congressional procedures are concerned. We should afford to Congress the presumption that it takes every precaution possible to avoid unnecessary damage to reputations. Some committees have codes of procedure, and others use the executive hearing technique to this end. The record in this case shows no conduct on the part of the Un-American Activities Committee that justifies condemnation. That there may have been such occasions is not for us to consider here. Nor should we permit its past transgressions, if any, to lead to the rigid restraint of all congressional committees. To carry on its heavy responsibility the compulsion of truth that does not incriminate is not only necessary to the Congress but is permitted within the limits of the Constitution.

One Person, One Vote
All Voters Are Created Equal
Reynolds v. Sims

No State shall deny to any person within its jurisdiction the equal protection of the laws. - The Constitution's Equal Protection Clause

The 1901 Alabama Constitution apportioned county representation in the State Legislature based on the 1900 Federal Census. Despite a requirement to reapportion the State Legislature every ten years in accordance with future Federal Censuses, Alabama made no changes in its apportionment over the next sixty years.

By the time of the 1960 Federal Census certain urban counties, which had grown in population over the preceding 60 years, were severely under-represented in the Alabama Legislature, while certain rural counties which had either decreased, stayed the same, or only slightly increased in population over the preceding 60 years were over-represented in the Alabama Legislature. In the Senate, Jefferson County, with a 1960 population of over 600,000, was apportioned only one seat, the same as Lowndes County, with a 1960 population of slightly over 15,000 - a disparity in representation of over 40-1. In the House, Mobile County, with a 1960 population of over 300,000, was apportioned only three seats, while Henry County, with a 1960 population of slightly over 15,000, was apportioned two seats - a disparity of 20-1.

On March 29, 1962 residents of Jefferson County (including M.O. Sims), alleging that the 1901 law was in violation of the Constitution's Equal Protection Clause, filed suit in Federal District Court against State officials (including B.A. Reynolds) to force reapportionment. On July 21, 1962 the District Court found the 1901 Alabama law unconstitutional and adopted a temporary reapportionment plan. When the State Legislature failed to enact a permanent reapportionment plan, the Court enacted one for them. Alabama, alleging that a Federal Court had no authority to reapportion a State Legislature, appealed to the United States Supreme Court.

On June 15, 1964 the 8-1 decision of the United States Supreme Court was announced by Chief Justice Earl Warren.

The *One Person, One Vote* Court

Chief Justice Earl Warren
Appointed Chief Justice by President Eisenhower
Served 1953 - 1969

Associate Justice Hugo Black
Appointed by President Franklin Roosevelt
Served 1937 - 1971

Associate Justice William O. Douglas
Appointed by President Franklin Roosevelt
Served 1939 - 1975

Associate Justice Tom Clark
Appointed by President Truman
Served 1949 - 1967

Associate Justice John Marshall Harlan
Appointed by President Eisenhower
Served 1955 - 1971

Associate Justice William Brennan
Appointed by President Eisenhower
Served 1956 - 1990

Associate Justice Potter Stewart
Appointed by President Eisenhower
Served 1958 - 1981

Associate Justice Byron White
Appointed by President Kennedy
Served 1962 - 1993

Associate Justice Abe Fortas
Appointed by President Lyndon Johnson
Served 1965 - 1969

The unedited legal text of *Reynolds v. Sims* can be found in volume 377 of *United States Reports* beginning on page 533. Our edited plain-English text follows.

Reynolds v. Sims
June 15, 1964

Chief Justice Earl Warren: Involved in these cases [is] a decision of the Federal District Court . . . holding invalid, under the Equal Protection Clause of the Federal Constitution, the existing and two legislatively proposed plans for the apportionment of seats in the two houses of the Alabama Legislature. . . .

On August 26, 1961, the original plaintiffs [parties making the charge] residents, taxpayers and voters of Jefferson County, Alabama [M.O. Sims and others], filed a complaint in the United States District Court . . . in their own behalf and on behalf of all similarly situated Alabama voters, challenging the apportionment of the Alabama Legislature. . . .

[Sims] alleged that the last apportionment of the Alabama Legislature was based on the 1900 federal census, despite the requirement of the State Constitution that the legislature be reapportioned decennially. They asserted that, since the population growth in the State from 1900 to 1960 had been uneven, Jefferson and other counties were now victims of serious discrimination with respect to the allocation of legislative representation. As a result of the failure of the legislature to reapportion itself, [Sims] asserted, they were denied "equal suffrage in free and equal elections . . . and the equal protection of the laws," in violation of the Alabama Constitution and the Fourteenth Amendment to the Federal Constitution. . . .

On July 12, 1962, an extraordinary session of the Alabama Legislature adopted two reapportionment plans to take effect for the 1966 elections. One was a proposed constitutional amendment, referred to as the "67-Senator Amendment." It provided for a House of Representatives consisting of 106 members, apportioned by giving one seat to each of Alabama's 67 counties and distributing the others according to population by the "equal proportions" method. . . .

The other reapportionment plan was embodied in a statutory measure adopted by the legislature and signed into law by the Alabama Governor, and was referred to as the "Crawford-Webb Act." It was enacted as standby legislation, to take effect in 1966 if the proposed constitutional amendment should fail of passage by a majority of the State's voters, or should the federal courts refuse to accept the proposed amendment (though not rejected by the voters) as effective action in compliance with the requirements of the Fourteenth Amendment. . . .

On July 21, 1962, the District Court held that the inequality of the existing representation in the Alabama Legislature violated the Equal Protection Clause of the Fourteenth Amendment, a finding which the Court noted had been "generally conceded" by the parties to the litigation, since population growth and shifts had converted the 1901 scheme, as perpetuated some 60 years later, into an invidiously discriminatory plan completely lacking in rationality. Under the existing provisions, applying 1960 census figures, only 25.1% of the State's total population resided in districts represented by a majority of the members of the Senate, and only 25.7% lived in counties which could elect a majority of the members of the House of Representatives. Population variance ratios of up to about 41-to-1 existed in the Senate, and up to about 16-to-1 in the House. . . .

The Court then considered both the proposed constitutional amendment and the Crawford-Webb Act to ascertain whether the legislature had taken effective action to remedy the unconstitutional aspects of the existing apportionment. . . .

The Court stated that the apportionment of one senator to each county, under the proposed constitutional amendment, would "make the discrimination in the Senate even more invidious than at present." . . .

Turning next to the provisions of the Crawford-Webb Act, the District Court found that its apportionment . . . was "totally unacceptable."

The District Court then directed its concern to the providing of an effective remedy. It indicated that it was adopting and ordering into effect for the November, 1962 election a provisional and temporary reapportionment plan composed of the provisions relating to the House of Representatives contained in the 67-Senator Amendment and the provisions of the Crawford-Webb Act relating to the Senate. . . .

[T]he Court emphasized that its "moderate" action was designed to break the stranglehold by the smaller counties on the Alabama Legislature, and would not suffice as a permanent reapportionment. . . .

Undeniably, the Constitution of the United States protects the right of all qualified citizens to vote, in state as well as in federal, elections. A consistent line of decisions by this Court in cases involving attempts to deny or restrict the right of suffrage has made this indelibly clear. It has been repeatedly recognized that all qualified voters have a constitutionally protected right to vote, and to have their votes counted. In *U.S. v. Mosley,* the Court stated that it is "as equally unquestionable that the right to have one's vote counted is as open to protection . . . as the right to put a ballot in a box." The right to vote can neither be denied outright, nor destroyed by alteration of ballots, nor diluted by ballot box stuffing. As the Court stated in *U.S. v. Classic,* "Obviously included within the right to choose, secured by the Constitution, is the right of qualified voters within a state to cast their ballots and have them counted. . . ." Racially based gerrymandering, and the conducting of white primaries, both of which result in denying to some citizens their right to vote, have been held to be constitutionally impermissible. And history has seen a continuing expansion of the scope of the right of suffrage in this country. The right to vote freely for the candidate of one's choice is of the essence of a democratic society, and any restrictions on that right strike at the heart of representative government. And the right of suffrage can be denied by a debasement or dilution of the weight of a citizen's vote just as effectively as by wholly prohibiting the free exercise of the franchise.

In *Baker v. Carr*, we held that a claim asserted under the Equal Protection Clause challenging the constitutionality of a State's apportionment of seats in its legislature, on the ground that the right to vote of certain citizens was effectively impaired, since debased and diluted, in effect presented a justiciable [substantial] controversy subject to adjudication [settlement] by federal courts. The spate of similar cases filed and decided by lower courts since our decision in *Baker* amply shows that the problem of state legislative malapportionment is one that is perceived to exist in a large number of the States. In *Baker*, a suit involving an attack on the apportionment of seats in the Tennessee Legislature, we remanded [returned] to the District Court, which had dismissed the action [suit]. . . . We intimated no view as to the proper constitutional standards for evaluating the validity of a state legislative apportionment scheme. Nor did we give any consideration to the question of appropriate remedies. Rather, we simply stated: "Beyond noting that we have no cause at this stage to doubt the District Court will be able to fashion relief if violations of constitutional rights are found, it is improper now to consider what remedy would be most appropriate if appellants prevail at the trial."

We indicated in *Baker*, however, that the Equal Protection Clause provides . . . standards for use by lower courts in determining the constitutionality of a state legislative apportionment scheme. . . .

In *Gray v. Sanders*, we held that the Georgia county unit system, applicable in statewide primary elections, was unconstitutional, since it resulted in a dilution of the weight of the votes of certain Georgia voters merely because of where they resided. After indicating that the Fifteenth and Nineteenth Amendments prohibit a State from overweighting or diluting votes on the basis of race or sex, we stated:

> "How, then, can one person be given twice or ten times the voting power of another person in a statewide election merely because he lives in a rural area or because he lives in the smallest rural county? Once the geographical unit for which a representative is to be chosen is designated, all who participate in the election are to have an equal vote - whatever their race, whatever their sex, whatever their occupation, whatever their income and wherever their home may be in that geographical unit. This is required by the Equal Protection Clause of the Fourteenth Amendment. The concept of 'we the people' under the Constitution visualizes no preferred class of voters, but equality among those who meet the basic qualifications. The idea that every voter is equal to every other voter in his State, when he casts his ballot in favor of one of several competing candidates, underlies many of our decisions."

Continuing, we stated that there is no indication in the Constitution that homesite or occupation affords a permissible basis for distinguishing between qualified voters within the State. And, finally, we concluded: "The conception of political equality from the Declaration of Independence, to

Lincoln's Gettysburg Address, to the Fifteenth, Seventeenth, and Nineteenth Amendments can mean only one thing - one person, one vote."

. . . . Legislators represent people, not trees or acres. Legislators are elected by voters, not farms or cities or economic interests. As long as ours is a representative form of government, and our legislatures are those instruments of government elected directly by and directly representative of the people, the right to elect legislators in a free and unimpaired fashion is a bedrock of our political system. It could hardly be gainsaid that a constitutional claim had been asserted by an allegation that certain otherwise qualified voters had been entirely prohibited from voting for members of their state legislature. And, if a State should provide that the votes of citizens in one part of the State should be given two times, or five times, or ten times the weight of votes of citizens in another part of the State, it could hardly be contended that the right to vote of those residing in the disfavored areas had not been effectively diluted. It would appear extraordinary to suggest that a State could be constitutionally permitted to enact a law providing that certain of the State's voters could vote two, five, or ten times for their legislative representatives, while voters living elsewhere could vote only once. And it is inconceivable that a state law to the effect that, in counting votes for legislators, the votes of citizens in one part of the State would be multiplied by two, five, or ten, while the votes of persons in another area would be counted only at face value, could be constitutionally sustainable [able to be approved]. Of course, the effect of state legislative districting schemes which give the same number of representatives to unequal numbers of constituents is identical. Overweighting and overvaluation of the votes of those living here has the certain effect of dilution and undervaluation of the votes of those living there. The resulting discrimination against those individual voters living in disfavored areas is easily demonstrable mathematically. Their right to vote is simply not the same right to vote as that of those living in a favored part of the State. Two, five, or ten of them must vote before the effect of their voting is equivalent to that of their favored neighbor. Weighting the votes of citizens differently, by any method or means, merely because of where they happen to reside, hardly seems justifiable. One must be ever aware that the Constitution forbids "sophisticated, as well as simple-minded, modes of discrimination." As we stated in *Wesberry v. Sanders,*

> "We do not believe that the Framers of the Constitution intended to permit the same vote-diluting discrimination to be accomplished through the device of districts containing widely varied numbers of inhabitants. To say that a vote is worth more in one district than in another would . . . run counter to our fundamental ideas of democratic government. . . ."

State legislatures are, historically, the fountainhead of representative government in this country. A number of them have their roots in colonial times, and substantially antedate the creation of our Nation and our Federal Government. In fact, the first formal stirrings of American political independence are to be found, in large part, in the views and actions of several of the colonial legislative bodies. With the birth of our National Government, and the adoption and ratification of the Federal Constitution, state legislatures retained a most important place in our Nation's governmental structure. But representative government is, in essence, self-government through the medium of elected representatives of the people, and each and every citizen has an inalienable right to full and effective participation in the political processes of his State's legislative bodies. Most citizens can achieve this participation only as qualified voters through the election of legislators to represent them. Full and effective participation by all citizens in state government requires, therefore, that each citizen have an equally effective voice in the election of members of his state legislature. Modern and viable state government needs, and the Constitution demands, no less.

Logically, in a society ostensibly grounded on representative government, it would seem reasonable that a majority of the people of a State could elect a majority of that State's legislators. To conclude differently, and to sanction minority control of state legislative bodies, would appear to deny majority rights in a way that far surpasses any possible denial of minority rights that might otherwise be thought to result. Since legislatures are responsible for enacting laws by which all citizens are to be governed, they should be bodies which are collectively responsive to the popular will. And the concept of equal protection has been traditionally viewed as requiring the uniform treatment of persons standing in the same relation to the governmental action questioned or challenged. With respect to the allocation of legislative representation, all voters, as citizens of a State, stand in the same relation regardless of where they live. Any suggested criteria for the differentiation of citizens are insufficient to justify any discrimination, as to the weight of their votes, unless relevant to the permissible purposes of legislative apportionment. Since the achieving of fair and effective representation for all citizens is concededly the basic aim of legislative apportionment, we conclude that the Equal Protection Clause guarantees the opportunity for equal participation by all voters in the election of state legislators. Diluting the weight of votes because of place of residence impairs basic constitutional rights under the Fourteenth Amendment just as much as invidious discriminations based upon factors such as race or economic status. Our constitutional system amply provides for the protection of minorities by means other than giving them majority control of state legislatures. And the democratic ideals of equality and majority rule, which have served this Nation so well in the past, are hardly of any less significance for the present and the future.

We are told that the matter of apportioning representation in a state legislature is a complex and many-faceted one. We are advised that States can rationally consider factors other than population in apportioning legislative representation. We are admonished not to restrict the power of the States to impose differing views as to political philosophy on their citizens. We are cautioned about the dangers of entering into political thickets and mathematical quagmires. Our answer is this: A denial of constitutionally protected rights demands judicial protection; our oath and our office require no less of us. . . .

To the extent that a citizen's right to vote is debased, he is that much less a citizen. The fact that an individual lives here or there is not a legitimate reason for overweighting or diluting the efficacy of his vote. The complexions of societies and civilizations change, often with amazing rapidity. A nation once primarily rural in character becomes predominantly urban. Representation schemes once fair and equitable become archaic and outdated. But the basic principle of representative government remains, and must remain, unchanged - the weight of a citizen's vote cannot be made to depend on where he lives. Population is, of necessity, the starting point for consideration and the controlling criterion for judgment in legislative apportionment controversies. A citizen, a qualified voter, is no more nor no less so because he lives in the city or on the farm. This is the clear and strong command of our Constitution's Equal Protection Clause. This is an essential part of the concept of a government of laws, and not men. This is at the heart of Lincoln's vision of "government of the people, by the people, [and] for the people." The Equal Protection Clause demands no less than substantially equal state legislative representation for all citizens, of all places as well as of all races.

We hold that, as a basic constitutional standard, the Equal Protection Clause requires that the seats in both houses of a bicameral state legislature must be apportioned on a population basis. Simply stated, an individual's right to vote for state legislators is unconstitutionally impaired when its weight is in a substantial fashion diluted when compared with votes of citizens living in other parts of the State. . . .

By holding that, as a federal constitutional requisite, both houses of a state legislature must be apportioned on a population basis, we mean that the Equal Protection Clause requires that a State make an honest and good faith effort to construct districts, in both houses of its legislature, as nearly of equal population as is practicable. We realize that it is a practical impossibility to arrange legislative districts so that each one has an identical number of residents, or citizens, or voters. Mathematical exactness or precision is hardly a workable constitutional requirement.

. . . . That the Equal Protection Clause requires that both houses of a state legislature be apportioned on a population basis does not mean that States cannot adopt some reasonable plan for periodic revision of their apportionment schemes. Decennial reapportionment appears to be a rational approach to readjustment of legislative representation in order to take into account population shifts and growth. Reallocation of legislative seats every ten years coincides with the prescribed practice in forty-one of the States, often honored more in the breach than the observance, however. Illustratively, the Alabama Constitution requires decennial reapportionment, yet the last reapportionment of the Alabama Legislature, when this suit was brought, was in 1901. Limitations on the frequency of reapportionment are justified by the need for stability and continuity in the organization of the legislative system, although undoubtedly reapportioning no more frequently than every ten years leads to some imbalance in the population of districts toward the end of the decennial period, and also to the development of resistance to change on the part of some incumbent legislators. In substance, we do not regard the Equal Protection Clause as requiring daily, monthly, annual or biennial reapportionment, so long as a State has a reasonably conceived plan for periodic readjustment of legislative representation. While we do not intend to indicate that decennial reapportionment is a constitutional requisite, compliance with such an approach would clearly meet the minimal requirements for maintaining a reasonably current scheme of legislative representation. And we do not mean to intimate that more frequent reapportionment would not be constitutionally permissible or practically desirable. But if reapportionment were accomplished with less frequency, it would assuredly be constitutionally suspect.

Although general provisions of the Alabama Constitution provide that the apportionment of seats in both houses of the Alabama Legislature should be on a population basis, other more detailed provisions clearly make compliance with both sets of requirements impossible. With respect to the operation of the Equal Protection Clause, it makes no difference whether a State's apportionment scheme is embodied in its constitution or in statutory provisions. In those States where the alleged malapportionment has resulted from noncompliance with state constitutional provisions which, if complied with, would result in an apportionment valid under the Equal Protection Clause, the judicial task of providing effective relief would appear to be rather simple. We agree with the view of the District Court that state constitutional provisions should be deemed violative of the Federal Constitution only when validly asserted constitutional rights could not otherwise be protected and effectuated. Clearly, courts should attempt to accommodate the relief ordered to the apportionment provisions of state constitutions insofar as is possible. But it is also quite clear that a state legislative apportionment scheme is no less violative of the Federal Constitution when it is based on state constitutional provisions which have been consistently complied with than when resulting from a noncompliance with state constitutional requirements. When there is an unavoidable conflict between the Federal and a State Constitution, the Supremacy Clause, of course, controls. . . . We feel that the District Court in this case acted in a most proper and commendable manner. It initially acted wisely in declining to stay [stop] the impending primary election in Alabama, and properly refrained from acting further until the Alabama Legislature had been given an opportunity to remedy the admitted discrepancies in the State's legislative apportionment scheme, while initially stating some of its views to provide guidelines for legislative action. And it correctly recognized that legislative reapportionment is primarily a matter for legislative consideration and determination, and that judicial relief becomes appropriate only when a legislature fails to reapportion according to federal constitutional requisites in a timely fashion after having had an adequate opportunity to do so. Additionally, the court below [the District Court] acted with proper judicial restraint, after the Alabama Legislature had failed to act effectively in remedying the constitutional deficiencies in the State's legislative apportionment scheme, in ordering its own temporary reapportionment plan into effect, at a time sufficiently early to permit the holding of elections pursuant to that plan without great difficulty, and in prescribing a plan admittedly provisional in purpose so as not to usurp the primary responsibility for reapportionment which rests with the legislature.

We find, therefore, that the action taken by the District Court in this case, in ordering into effect a reapportionment of both houses of the Alabama Legislature for purposes of the 1962 primary and general elections, by using the best parts of the two proposed plans which it had found, as a whole, to be invalid, was an appropriate and well considered exercise of judicial power. Admittedly, the lower court's ordered plan was intended only as a temporary and provisional measure, and the District Court correctly indicated that the plan was invalid as a permanent apportionment. In retaining jurisdiction [legal right] while deferring a hearing on the issuance of a final injunction [court order stopping an action] in order to give the provisionally reapportioned legislature an opportunity to act effectively, the court below proceeded in a proper fashion. Since the District Court evinced its realization that its ordered reapportionment could not be sustained as the basis for conducting the 1966 election of Alabama legislators, and avowedly intends to take some further action should the reapportioned Alabama Legislature fail to enact a constitutionally valid, permanent apportionment scheme in the interim, we affirm [uphold] the judgment below and remand the cases for further proceedings consistent with the views stated in this opinion.

The Constitution And The Right To Die
Physician-Assisted Suicide And The Law
Washington State v. Glucksberg
New York State v. Quill

A person is guilty of promoting a suicide attempt when he knowingly causes or aids another person to attempt suicide.
- Washington State's Promoting Suicide Law

A person is guilty of manslaughter when he intentionally aids another person to commit suicide. A person is guilty of promoting a suicide attempt when he knowingly causes or aids another person to attempt suicide.
- New York State's Aiding and Promoting Suicide Law

On January 29, 1994 a right-to-die coalition (including Dr. Harold Glucksberg) filed suit in U.S. District Court seeking to overturn Washington State's "Promoting Suicide Law" as it applied specifically to criminal prohibitions on physician-assisted suicide by mentally competent, terminally ill adults in the final stages of their illnesses. On March 6, 1996 the U.S. Ninth Circuit Court of Appeals held Washington State's "Promoting Suicide Law" to be in violation of the Constitution's Due Process Clause. Washington appealed to the United States Supreme Court.

On July 20, 1994 a right-to-die coalition (including Dr. Timothy Quill) filed suit in U.S. District Court seeking to overturn New York State's "Aiding and Promoting Suicide Law" as it applied specifically to criminal prohibitions on physician-assisted suicide by mentally competent, terminally ill adults in the final stages of their illnesses. On April 2, 1996 the U.S. Second Circuit Court of Appeals held New York State's "Aiding and Promoting Suicide Law" to be in violation of the Constitution's Equal Protection Clause. New York appealed to the United States Supreme Court.

On June 26, 1997 the U.S. Supreme Court issued a 9-0 decision in the *Washington State v. Glucksberg* Due Process and the Right-To-Die case, and a 9-0 decision in the *New York State v. Quill* Equal Protection and the Right-To-Die case. Both decisions were announced by Chief Justice William Rehnquist.

The *Constitution And The Right To Die* Court

Chief Justice William Rehnquist
Appointed Chief Justice by President Reagan
Appointed Associate Justice by President Nixon
Served 1971 -

Associate Justice John Paul Stevens
Appointed by President Ford
Served 1975 -

Associate Justice Sandra Day O'Connor
Appointed by President Reagan
Served 1981 -

Associate Justice Antonin Scalia
Appointed by President Reagan
Served 1986 -

Associate Justice Anthony Kennedy
Appointed by President Reagan
Served 1988 -

Associate Justice David Souter
Appointed by President Bush
Served 1990 -

Associate Justice Clarence Thomas
Appointed by President Bush
Served 1991 -

Associate Justice Ruth Bader Ginsberg
Appointed by President Clinton
Served 1993 -

Associate Justice Stephen Breyer
Appointed by President Clinton
Served 1994 -

The unedited legal text of *Washington State v. Glucksberg* and *New York State v. Quill* can be found in volume 521 of *United States Reports*. Our edited plain-English text follows.

Washington State v. Glucksberg
June 26, 1997

Chief Justice William Rehnquist: The question presented in this case is whether Washington's prohibition against "caus[ing]" or "aid[ing]" a suicide offends the Fourteenth Amendment to the United States Constitution. We hold that it does not.

It has always been a crime to assist a suicide in the State of Washington. In 1854, Washington's first Territorial Legislature outlawed "assisting another in the commission of self-murder." Today, Washington law provides: "A person is guilty of promoting a suicide attempt when he knowingly causes or aids another person to attempt suicide." "Promoting a suicide attempt" is a felony, punishable by up to five years' imprisonment and up to a $10,000 fine. At the same time, Washington's Natural Death Act, enacted in 1979, states that the "withholding or withdrawal of life-sustaining treatment" at a patient's direction "shall not, for any purpose, constitute a suicide."

Petitioners [parties making a charge] in this case are the State of Washington and its Attorney General. Respondents [parties charged with an act] Harold Glucksberg, M.D., Abigail Halperin, M.D., Thomas A. Preston, M.D., and Peter Shalit, M.D., are physicians who practice in Washington. These doctors occasionally treat terminally ill, suffering patients, and declare that they would assist these patients in ending their lives if not for Washington's assisted-suicide ban. In January 1994, [the doctors], along with three gravely ill, pseudonymous plaintiffs who have since died, and Compassion in Dying, a nonprofit organization that counsels people considering physician-assisted suicide, sued in the United States District Court, seeking a declaration that [the Washington law prohibiting physician-assisted suicide] is . . . unconstitutional.

The plaintiffs asserted "the existence of a liberty interest protected by the Fourteenth Amendment which extends to a personal choice by a mentally competent, terminally ill adult to commit physician-assisted suicide." Relying primarily on *Planned Parenthood v. Casey* and *Cruzan v. Director, Missouri Department of Health*, the District Court agreed, and concluded that Washington's assisted-suicide ban is unconstitutional because it "places an undue burden on the exercise of [that] constitutionally protected liberty interest." The District Court also decided that the Washington statute violated the Equal Protection Clause's requirement that "all persons similarly situated . . . be treated alike."

A panel of the Court of Appeals for the Ninth Circuit reversed, emphasizing that "[i]n the two hundred and five years of our existence no constitutional right to aid in killing oneself has ever been asserted and upheld by a court of final jurisdiction." The Ninth Circuit reheard the case en banc [with the entire court participating in the decision], reversed the panel's decision, and affirmed [upheld] the District Court. Like the District Court, the en banc Court of Appeals emphasized our *Casey* and *Cruzan* decisions. The court also discussed what it described as "historical" and "current societal attitudes" toward suicide and assisted suicide, and concluded that "the Constitution encompasses a due process liberty interest in controlling the time and manner of one's death - that there is, in short, a constitutionally-recognized right to die. After "[w]eighing and then balancing" this interest against Washington's various interests, the court held that the State's assisted-suicide ban was unconstitutional "as applied to terminally ill competent adults who wish to hasten their deaths with medication prescribed by their physicians." The court did not reach the District Court's equal-protection holding. We granted certiorari [agreed to hear the case], and now reverse.

We begin, as we do in all due process cases, by examining our Nation's history, legal traditions, and practices. In almost every State - indeed, in almost every western democracy - it is a crime to assist a suicide. The States' assisted-suicide bans are not innovations. Rather, they are long-standing expressions of the States' commitment to the protection and preservation of all human life. Indeed, opposition to and condemnation of suicide - and, therefore, of assisting suicide - are consistent and enduring themes of our philosophical, legal, and cultural heritages.

More specifically, for over 700 years, the Anglo-American common law tradition [that established by usage and custom] has punished or otherwise disapproved of both suicide and assisting suicide. In the 13th century, Henry de Bracton, one of the first legal-treatise writers, observed that "[j]ust as a man may commit felony [serious crime] by slaying another so may he do so by slaying himself." The real and personal property of one who killed himself to avoid conviction and punishment for a crime were forfeit to the king; however, thought Bracton, "if a man slays himself in weariness of life or because he is unwilling to endure further bodily pain . . . [only] his movable goods [were] confiscated." Thus, "[t]he principle that suicide of a sane person, for whatever reason, was a punishable felony was . . . introduced into English common law." Centuries later, Sir William Blackstone, whose *Commentaries on the Laws of England* not only provided a definitive summary of the common law but was also a primary legal authority for 18th and 19th century American lawyers, referred to suicide as "self-murder" and "the pretended heroism, but real cowardice, of the Stoic philosophers, who destroyed themselves to avoid those ills which they had not the fortitude to endure. . . ." Blackstone emphasized that "the law has . . . ranked [suicide] among the highest crimes," although, anticipating later developments, he conceded that the harsh and shameful punishments imposed for suicide "borde[r] a little upon severity."

For the most part, the early American colonies adopted the common-law approach. For example, the legislators of the Providence Plantations, which would later become Rhode Island, declared, in 1647, that "[s]elf-murder is by all agreed to be the most unnatural, and it is by this present Assembly declared, to be that, wherein he that doth it, kills himself out of a premeditated hatred against his own life or other humor: . . . his goods and chattels are the king's custom, but not his debts nor lands; but in case he be an infant, a lunatic, mad or distracted man, he forfeits nothing." Virginia also required ignominious burial for suicides, and their estates were forfeit to the crown.

Over time, however, the American colonies abolished these harsh common-law penalties. William Penn abandoned the criminal-forfeiture sanction in Pennsylvania in 1701, and the other colonies (and later, the other States) eventually followed this example. Zephaniah Swift who would later become Chief Justice of Connecticut, wrote in 1796 that

> "[t]here can be no act more contemptible, than to attempt to punish an offender for a crime, by exercising a mean act of revenge upon lifeless clay, that is insensible of the punishment. There can be no greater cruelty than the inflicting [of] a punishment, as the forfeiture of goods, which must fall solely on the innocent offspring of the offender. . . . [Suicide] is so abhorrent to the feelings of mankind, and that strong love of life which is implanted in the human heart, that it cannot be so frequently committed, as to become dangerous to society. There can of course be no necessity of any punishment."

This statement makes it clear, however, that the movement away from the common law's harsh sanctions did not represent an acceptance of suicide; rather, as Chief Justice Swift observed, this change reflected the growing consensus that it was unfair to punish the suicide's family for his wrongdoing. Nonetheless, although States moved away from Blackstone's treatment of suicide, courts continued to condemn it as a grave public wrong.

That suicide remained a grievous, though nonfelonious, wrong is confirmed by the fact that colonial and early state legislatures and courts did not retreat from prohibiting assisting suicide. Swift, in his early 19th century treatise on the laws of Connecticut, stated that "[i]f one counsels another to commit suicide, and the other by reason of the advice kills himself, the advisor is guilty of murder as principal." This was the well established common-law view, as was the similar principle that the consent of a homicide victim is "wholly immaterial to the guilt of the person who cause[d] his death." And the prohibitions against assisting suicide never contained exceptions for those who were near death. Rather, "[t]he life of those to whom life ha[d] become a burden - of those who [were] hopelessly diseased or fatally wounded - nay, even the lives of criminals condemned to death, [were] under the protection of law, equally as the lives of those who [were] in the full tide of life's enjoyment, and anxious to continue to live."

The earliest American statute explicitly to outlaw assisting suicide was enacted in New York in 1828, and many of the new States and Territories followed New York's example. Between 1857 and 1865, a New York commission led by Dudley Field drafted a criminal code that prohibited "aiding" a suicide and, specifically, "furnish[ing] another person with any deadly weapon or poisonous drug, knowing that such person intends to use such weapon or drug in taking his own life." By the time the Fourteenth Amendment was ratified, it was a crime in most States to assist a suicide. The Field Penal Code was adopted in the Dakota Territory in 1877, in New York in 1881, and its language served as a model for several other western States' statutes in the late 19th and early 20th centuries. California, for example, codified its assisted-suicide prohibition in 1874, using language similar to the Field Code's. In this century, the Model Penal Code also prohibited "aiding" suicide, prompting many States to enact or revise their assisted-suicide bans. The Code's drafters observed that "the interests in the sanctity of life that are represented by the criminal homicide laws are threatened by one who expresses a willingness to participate in taking the life of another, even though the act may be accomplished with the consent, or at the request, of the suicide victim."

Though deeply rooted, the States' assisted-suicide bans have in recent years been reexamined and, generally, reaffirmed. Because of advances in medicine and technology, Americans today are increasingly likely to die in institutions, from chronic illnesses. Public concern and democratic action are therefore sharply focused on how best to protect dignity and independence at the end of life, with the result that there have been many significant changes in state laws and in the attitudes these laws reflect. Many States, for example, now permit "living wills," surrogate health-care decisionmaking, and the withdrawal or refusal of life-sustaining medical treatment. At the same time, however, voters and legislators continue for the most part to reaffirm their States' prohibitions on assisting suicide.

The Washington statute at issue in this case was enacted in 1975 as part of a revision of that State's criminal code. Four years later, Washington passed its Natural Death Act, which specifically stated that the "withholding or withdrawal of life-sustaining treatment . . . shall not, for any purpose, constitute a suicide" and that "[n]othing in this chapter shall be construed [interpreted] to condone, authorize, or approve mercy killing. . . ." In 1991, Washington voters rejected a ballot initiative which, had it passed, would have permitted a form of physician-assisted suicide. Washington then added a provision to the Natural Death Act expressly excluding physician-assisted suicide.

California voters rejected an assisted-suicide initiative similar to Washington's in 1993. On the other hand, in 1994, voters in Oregon enacted, also through ballot initiative, that State's "Death With Dignity Act," which legalized physician-assisted suicide for competent, terminally ill adults. Since the Oregon vote, many proposals to legalize assisted-suicide have been and continue to be introduced in the States' legislatures, but none has been enacted. And just last year, Iowa and Rhode Island joined the overwhelming majority of States explicitly prohibiting assisted suicide. Also, on April 30, 1997, President Clinton signed the Federal Assisted Suicide Funding Restriction Act of 1997, which prohibits the use of federal funds in support of physician-assisted suicide.

Thus, the States are currently engaged in serious, thoughtful examinations of physician-assisted suicide and other similar issues. For example, New York State's Task Force on Life and the Law - an ongoing, blue-ribbon commission composed of doctors, ethicists, lawyers, religious leaders, and interested laymen - was convened in 1984 and commissioned with "a broad mandate to recommend public policy on issues raised by medical advances." Over the past decade, the Task Force has recommended laws relating to end-of-life decisions, surrogate pregnancy, and organ donation. After studying physician-assisted suicide, however, the Task Force unanimously concluded that "[l]egalizing assisted suicide and euthanasia would pose profound risks to many individuals who are ill and vulnerable. . . . [T]he potential dangers of this dramatic change in public policy would outweigh any benefit that might be achieved."

Attitudes toward suicide itself have changed since Bracton, but our laws have consistently condemned, and continue to prohibit, assisting suicide. Despite changes in medical technology and notwithstanding an increased emphasis on the importance of end-of-life decisionmaking, we have not retreated from this prohibition. Against this backdrop of history, tradition, and practice, we now turn to respondents' constitutional claim.

The Due Process Clause guarantees more than fair process, and the "liberty" it protects includes more than the absence of physical restraint. The Clause also provides heightened protection against government interference with certain fundamental rights and liberty interests. In a long line of cases, we have held that, in addition to the specific freedoms protected by the Bill of Rights, the "liberty" specially protected by the Due Process Clause includes the rights to marry, to have children, to direct the education and upbringing of one's children, to marital privacy, to use contraception, to bodily integrity, and to abortion. We have also assumed, and strongly suggested, that the Due Process Clause protects the traditional right to refuse unwanted life-saving medical treatment.

But we "ha[ve] always been reluctant to expand the concept of substantive due process because guideposts for responsible decisionmaking in this uncharted area are scarce and open-ended." By extending constitutional protection to an asserted right or liberty interest, we, to a great extent, place the matter outside the arena of public debate and legislative action. We must therefore "exercise the utmost care whenever we are asked to break new ground in this field," lest the liberty protected by the Due Process Clause be subtly transformed into the policy preferences of the members of this Court.

Our established method of substantive due process analysis has two primary features: First, we have regularly observed that the Due Process Clause specially protects those fundamental rights and liberties which are, objectively, "deeply rooted in this Nation's history and tradition," and "implicit in the concept of ordered liberty"; such that "neither liberty nor justice would exist if they were sacrificed." Second, we have required in substantive due process cases a "careful description" of the asserted fundamental liberty interest. Our Nation's history, legal traditions, and practices thus provide the crucial "guideposts for responsible decisionmaking" that direct and restrain our exposition of the Due Process Clause. As we stated recently in *Reno v. Flores,* the Fourteenth Amendment "forbids the government to infringe . . . 'fundamental' liberty interests at all, no matter what process is provided, unless the infringement is narrowly tailored to serve a compelling state interest."

. . . . Turning to the claim at issue here, the Court of Appeals stated that "[p]roperly analyzed, the first issue to be resolved is whether there is a liberty interest in determining the time and manner of one's death," or, in other words, "[i]s there a right to die?" Similarly, respondents assert a "liberty to choose how to die" and a right to "control of one's final days," and describe the asserted liberty as "the right to choose a humane, dignified death," and "the liberty to shape death." As noted above, we have a tradition of carefully formulating the interest at stake in substantive due process cases. For example, although *Cruzan* is often described as a "right to die" case, we were, in fact, more precise: we assumed that the Constitution granted competent persons a "constitutionally protected right to refuse lifesaving hydration and nutrition." The Washington statute at issue in this case prohibits "aid[ing] another person to attempt suicide," and, thus, the question before us is whether the "liberty" specially protected by the Due Process Clause includes a right to commit suicide which itself includes a right to assistance in doing so.

We now inquire whether this asserted right has any place in our Nation's traditions. Here, as discussed above, we are confronted with a consistent and almost universal tradition that has long rejected the asserted right, and continues explicitly to reject it today, even for terminally ill, mentally competent adults. To hold for respondents, we would have to reverse centuries of legal doctrine and practice, and strike down the considered policy choice of almost every State.

Respondents contend, however, that the liberty interest they assert is consistent with this Court's substantive due process line of cases, if not with this Nation's history and practice. Pointing to *Casey* and *Cruzan*, respondents read our jurisprudence [philosophy of law] in this area as reflecting a general tradition of "self-sovereignty;" and as teaching that the "liberty" protected by the Due Process Clause includes "basic and intimate exercises of personal autonomy." According to respondents, our liberty jurisprudence, and the broad, individualistic principles it reflects, protects the "liberty of competent, terminally ill adults to make end-of-life decisions free of undue government interference." The question presented in this case, however, is whether the protections of the Due Process Clause include a right to commit suicide with another's assistance. With this "careful description" of respondents' claim in mind, we turn to *Casey* and *Cruzan*.

In *Cruzan*, we considered whether Nancy Beth Cruzan, who had been severely injured in an automobile accident and was in a persistent vegetative state, "ha[d] a right under the United States Constitution which would require the hospital to withdraw life-sustaining treatment" at her parents' request. We began with the observation that "[a]t common law, even the touching of one person by another without consent and without legal justification was a battery." We then discussed the related rule that "informed consent is generally required for medical treatment." After reviewing a long line of relevant state cases, we concluded that "the common-law doctrine of informed consent is viewed as generally encompassing the right of a competent individual to refuse medical treatment." Next, we reviewed our own cases on the subject, and stated that "[t]he principle that a competent person has a constitutionally protected liberty interest in refusing unwanted medical treatment may be inferred from our prior decisions." Therefore, "for purposes of [that] case, we assume[d] that the United States Constitution would grant a competent person a constitutionally protected right to refuse lifesaving hydration and nutrition." We concluded that, notwithstanding this right, the Constitution permitted Missouri to require clear and convincing evidence of an incompetent patient's wishes concerning the withdrawal of life-sustaining treatment.

Respondents contend that in *Cruzan* we "acknowledged that competent, dying persons have the right to direct the removal of life-sustaining medical treatment and thus hasten death," and that "the constitutional principle behind recognizing the patient's liberty to direct the withdrawal of artificial life support applies at least as strongly to the choice to hasten impending death by consuming lethal medication." Similarly, the Court of Appeals concluded that "*Cruzan*, by recognizing a liberty interest that includes the refusal of artificial provision of life-sustaining food and water, necessarily recognize[d] a liberty interest in hastening one's own death."

The right assumed in *Cruzan*, however, was not simply deduced from abstract concepts of personal autonomy. Given the common-law rule that forced medication was a battery, and the long legal tradition protecting the decision to refuse unwanted medical treatment, our assumption was entirely consistent with this Nation's history and constitutional traditions. The decision to commit suicide with the assistance of another may be just as personal and profound as the decision to refuse unwanted medical treatment, but it has never enjoyed similar legal protection. Indeed, the two acts are widely and reasonably regarded as quite distinct. In *Cruzan* itself, we recognized that most States outlawed assisted suicide - and even more do today - and we certainly gave no intimation that the right to refuse unwanted medical treatment could be somehow transmuted into a right to assistance in committing suicide.

Respondents also rely on *Casey.* There, the Court's opinion concluded that "the essential holding of *Roe v. Wade* should be retained and once again reaffirmed." We held, first, that a woman has a right, before her fetus is viable, to an abortion "without undue interference from the State"; second, that States may restrict post-viability abortions, so long as exceptions are made to protect a woman's life and health; and third, that the State has legitimate interests throughout a pregnancy in protecting the health of the woman and the life of the unborn child. In reaching this conclusion, the opinion discussed in some detail this Court's substantive due process tradition of interpreting the Due Process Clause to protect certain fundamental rights and "personal decisions relating to marriage, procreation, contraception, family relationships, child rearing and education," and noted that many of those rights and liberties "involv[e] the most intimate and personal choices a person may make in a lifetime."

The Court of Appeals, like the District Court, found *Casey* "highly instructive" and "almost prescriptive" for determining "what liberty interest may inhere in a terminally ill person's choice to commit suicide": "Like the decision of whether or not to have an abortion, the decision how and when to die is one of 'the most intimate and personal choices a person may make in a lifetime,' a choice 'central to personal dignity and autonomy.'"

Similarly, respondents emphasize the statement in *Casey* that:

> "At the heart of liberty is the right to define one's own concept of existence, of meaning, of the universe, and of the mystery of human life. Beliefs about these matters could not define the attributes of personhood were they formed under compulsion of the State."

By choosing this language, the Court's opinion in *Casey* described, in a general way and in light of our prior cases, those personal activities and decisions that this Court has identified as so deeply rooted in our history and traditions, or so fundamental to our concept of constitutionally ordered liberty, that they are protected by the Fourteenth Amendment. The opinion moved from the recognition that liberty necessarily includes freedom of conscience and belief about ultimate considerations to the observation that "though the abortion decision may originate within the zone of conscience and belief, it is more than a philosophic exercise." That many of the rights and liberties protected by the Due Process Clause sound in personal autonomy does not warrant the sweeping conclusion that any and all important, intimate, and personal decisions are so protected, and *Casey* did not suggest otherwise.

The history of the law's treatment of assisted suicide in this country has been and continues to be one of the rejection of nearly all efforts to permit it. That being the case, our decisions lead us to conclude that the asserted "right" to assistance in committing suicide is not a fundamental liberty interest protected by the Due Process Clause. The Constitution also requires, however, that Washington's assisted-suicide ban be rationally related to legitimate government interests. This requirement is unquestionably met here. As the court below [the Court of Appeals] recognized, Washington's assisted-suicide ban implicates a number of state interests.

First, Washington has an "unqualified interest in the preservation of human life." The State's prohibition on assisted suicide, like all homicide laws, both reflects and advances its commitment to this interest. This interest is symbolic and aspirational as well as practical:

> "While suicide is no longer prohibited or penalized, the ban against assisted suicide and euthanasia shores up the notion of limits in human relationships. It reflects the gravity with which we view the decision to take one's own life or the life of another, and our reluctance to encourage or promote these decisions."

Respondents admit that "[t]he State has a real interest in preserving the lives of those who can still contribute to society and enjoy life." The Court of Appeals also recognized Washington's interest in protecting life, but held that the "weight" of this interest depends on the "medical condition and the wishes of the person whose life is at stake." Washington, however, has rejected this sliding-scale approach and, through its assisted-suicide ban, insists that all persons' lives, from beginning to end, regardless of physical or mental condition, are under the full protection of the law. As we have previously affirmed, the States "may properly decline to make judgments about the 'quality' of life that a particular individual may enjoy." This remains true, as *Cruzan* makes clear, even for those who are near death.

Relatedly, all admit that suicide is a serious public-health problem, especially among persons in otherwise vulnerable groups. The State has an interest in preventing suicide, and in studying, identifying, and treating its causes.

Those who attempt suicide - terminally ill or not - often suffer from depression or other mental disorders. Research indicates, however, that many people who request physician-assisted suicide withdraw that request if their depression and pain are treated. The New York Task Force, however, expressed its concern that, because depression is difficult to diagnose, physicians and medical professionals often fail to respond adequately to seriously ill patients' needs. Thus, legal physician-assisted suicide could make it more difficult for the State to protect depressed or mentally ill persons, or those who are suffering from untreated pain, from suicidal impulses.

The State also has an interest in protecting the integrity and ethics of the medical profession. In contrast to the Court of Appeals' conclusion that "the integrity of the medical profession would [not] be threatened in any way by [physician-assisted suicide]," the American Medical Association, like many other medical and physicians' groups, has concluded that "[p]hysician-assisted suicide is fundamentally incompatible with the physician's role as healer." And physician-assisted suicide could, it is argued, undermine the trust that is essential to the doctor-patient relationship by blurring the time-honored line between healing and harming.

Next, the State has an interest in protecting vulnerable groups - including the poor, the elderly, and disabled persons - from abuse, neglect, and mistakes. The Court of Appeals dismissed the State's concern that disadvantaged persons might be pressured into physician-assisted suicide as "ludicrous on its face." We have recognized, however, the real risk of subtle coercion and undue influence in end-of-life situations. Similarly, the New York Task Force warned that "[l]egalizing physician-assisted suicide would pose profound risks to many individuals who are ill and vulnerable. . . . The risk of harm is greatest for the many individuals in our society whose autonomy and well-being are already compromised by poverty, lack of access to good medical care, advanced age, or membership in a stigmatized social group." If physician-assisted suicide were permitted, many might resort to it to spare their families the substantial financial burden of end-of-life health-care costs.

The State's interest here goes beyond protecting the vulnerable from coercion; it extends to protecting disabled and terminally ill people from prejudice, negative and inaccurate stereotypes, and "societal indifference." The State's assisted-suicide ban reflects and reinforces its policy that the lives of terminally ill, disabled, and elderly people must be no less valued than the lives of the young and healthy, and that a seriously disabled person's suicidal impulses should be interpreted and treated the same way as anyone else's.

Finally, the State may fear that permitting assisted suicide will start it down the path to voluntary and perhaps even involuntary euthanasia. The Court of Appeals struck down Washington's assisted-suicide ban only "as applied to competent, terminally ill adults who wish to hasten their deaths by obtaining medication prescribed by their doctors." Washington insists, however, that the impact of the court's decision will not and cannot be so limited. If suicide is protected as a matter of constitutional right, it is argued, "every man and woman in the United States must enjoy it." The Court of Appeals' decision, and its expansive reasoning, provide ample support for the State's concerns. The court noted, for example, that the "decision of a duly appointed surrogate decisionmaker is for all legal purposes the decision of the patient himself"; that "in some instances, the patient may be unable to self-administer the drugs and . . . administration by the physician . . . may be the only way the patient may be able to receive them"; and that not only physicians, but also family members and loved ones, will inevitably participate in assisting suicide. Thus, it turns out that what is couched as a limited right to "physician-assisted suicide" is likely, in effect, a much broader license, which could prove extremely difficult to police and contain. Washington's ban on assisting suicide prevents such erosion.

This concern is further supported by evidence about the practice of euthanasia in the Netherlands. The Dutch government's own study revealed that in 1990, there were 2,300 cases of voluntary euthanasia (defined as "the deliberate termination of another's life at his request"), 400 cases of assisted suicide, and more than 1,000 cases of euthanasia without an explicit request. In addition to these latter 1,000 cases, the study found an additional 4,941 cases where physicians administered lethal morphine overdoses without the patients' explicit consent. This study suggests that, despite the existence of various reporting procedures, euthanasia in the Netherlands has not been limited to competent, terminally ill adults who are enduring physical suffering, and that regulation of the practice may not have prevented abuses in cases involving vulnerable persons, including severely disabled neonates and elderly persons suffering from dementia. The New York Task Force, citing the Dutch experience, observed that "assisted suicide and euthanasia are closely linked," and concluded that the "risk of . . . abuse is neither speculative nor distant." Washington, like most other States, reasonably ensures against this risk by banning, rather than regulating, assisting suicide.

We need not weigh exactingly the relative strengths of these various interests. They are unquestionably important and legitimate, and Washington's ban on assisted suicide is at least reasonably related to their promotion and protection.

We therefore hold that [the Washington statute prohibiting physician-assisted suicide] does not violate the Fourteenth Amendment . . . "as applied to competent, terminally ill adults who wish to hasten their deaths by obtaining medication prescribed by their doctors."

Throughout the Nation, Americans are engaged in an earnest and profound debate about the morality, legality, and practicality of physician-assisted suicide. Our holding permits this debate to continue, as it should in a democratic society. The decision of the en banc Court of Appeals is reversed, and the case is remanded [sent back to the lower court] for further proceedings consistent with this opinion.

New York State v. Quill
June 26, 1997

Chief Justice William Rehnquist: In New York, as in most States, it is a crime to aid another to commit or attempt suicide, but patients may refuse even lifesaving medical treatment. The question presented by this case is whether New York's prohibition on assisting suicide therefore violates the Equal Protection Clause of the Fourteenth Amendment. We hold that it does not.

Petitioners [parties making a charge] are various New York public officials. Respondents [parties charged with an act] Timothy E. Quill, Samuel C. Klagsbrun, and Howard A. Grossman are physicians who practice in New York. They assert that although it would be "consistent with the standards of [their] medical practice[s]" to prescribe lethal medication for "mentally competent, terminally ill patients" who are suffering great pain and desire a doctor's help in taking their own lives, they are deterred from doing so by New York's ban on assisting suicide. Respondents, and three gravely ill patients who have since died, sued the State's Attorney General in the United States District Court. They urged that because New York permits a competent person to refuse life-sustaining medical treatment, and because the refusal of such treatment is "essentially the same thing" as physician-assisted suicide, New York's assisted-suicide ban violates the Equal Protection Clause.

The District Court disagreed: "[I]t is hardly unreasonable or irrational for the State to recognize a difference between allowing nature to take its course, even in the most severe situations, and intentionally using an artificial death - producing device." The court noted New York's "obvious legitimate interests in preserving life, and in protecting vulnerable persons," and concluded that "[u]nder the United States Constitution and the federal system it establishes, the resolution of this issue is left to the normal democratic processes within the State."

The Court of Appeals for the Second Circuit reversed. The court determined that, despite the assisted-suicide ban's apparent general applicability, "New York law does not treat equally all competent persons who are in the final stages of fatal illness and wish to hasten their deaths," because "those in the final stages of terminal illness who are on life-support systems are allowed to hasten their deaths by directing the removal of such systems, but those who are similarly situated, except for the previous attachment of life-sustaining equipment, are not allowed to hasten death by self-administering prescribed drugs." In the court's view, "[t]he ending of life by [the withdrawal of life-support systems] is nothing more nor less than assisted suicide." The Court of Appeals then examined whether this supposed unequal treatment was rationally related to any legitimate state interests, and concluded that "to the extent that [New York's statutes] prohibit a physician from prescribing medications to be self-administered by a mentally competent, terminally-ill person in the final stages of his terminal illness, they are not rationally related to any legitimate state interest." We granted certiorari [agreed to hear the case], and now reverse.

The Equal Protection Clause commands that no State shall "deny to any person within its jurisdiction the equal protection of the laws." This provision creates no substantive rights. Instead, it embodies a general rule that States must treat like cases alike but may treat unlike cases accordingly. If a legislative classification or distinction "neither burdens a fundamental right nor targets a suspect class, we will uphold [it] so long as it bears a rational relation to some legitimate end."

New York's statutes outlawing assisting suicide affect and address matters of profound significance to all New Yorkers alike. They neither infringe fundamental rights nor involve suspect classifications. These laws are therefore entitled to a "strong presumption of validity."

. . . [N]either New York's ban on assisting suicide nor its statutes permitting patients to refuse medical treatment treat anyone differently than anyone else or draw any distinctions between persons. Everyone, regardless of physical condition, is entitled, if competent, to refuse unwanted lifesaving medical treatment; no one is permitted to assist a suicide. Generally speaking, laws that apply evenhandedly to all "unquestionably comply" with the Equal Protection Clause.

The Court of Appeals, however, concluded that some terminally ill people - those who are on life-support systems - are treated differently than those who are not, in that the former may "hasten death" by ending treatment, but the latter may not "hasten death" through physician-assisted suicide. This conclusion depends on the submission that ending or refusing lifesaving medical treatment "is nothing more nor less than assisted suicide." Unlike the Court of Appeals, we think the distinction between assisting suicide and withdrawing life-sustaining treatment, a distinction widely recognized and endorsed in the medical profession and in our legal traditions, is both important and logical; it is certainly rational.

The distinction comports with fundamental legal principles of causation and intent. First, when a patient refuses life-sustaining medical treatment, he dies from an underlying fatal disease or pathology; but if a patient ingests lethal medication prescribed by a physician, he is killed by that medication.

Furthermore, a physician who withdraws, or honors a patient's refusal to begin life-sustaining medical treatment purposefully intends, or may so intend, only to respect his patient's wishes and "to cease doing useless and futile or degrading things to the patient when [the patient] no longer stands to benefit from them." The same is true when a doctor provides aggressive palliative care; in some cases, painkilling drugs may hasten a patient's death, but the physician's purpose and intent is, or may be, only to ease his patient's pain. A doctor who assists a suicide, however, "must, necessarily and indubitably, intend primarily that the patient be made dead." Similarly, a patient who commits suicide with a doctor's aid necessarily has the specific intent to end his or her own life, while a patient who refuses or discontinues treatment might not.

The law has long used actors' intent or purpose to distinguish between two acts that may have the same result. Put differently, the law distinguishes actions taken "because of" a given end from actions taken "in spite of" their unintended but foreseen consequences.

Given these general principles, it is not surprising that many courts, including New York courts, have carefully distinguished refusing life-sustaining treatment from suicide. In fact, the first state-court decision explicitly to authorize withdrawing lifesaving treatment noted the "real distinction between the self-infliction of deadly harm and a self-determination against artificial life support." And recently, the Michigan Supreme Court also rejected the argument that the distinction "between acts that artificially sustain life and acts that artificially curtail life" is merely a "distinction without constitutional significance - a meaningless exercise in semantic gymnastics," insisting that "the *Cruzan* majority disagreed and so do we."

Similarly, the overwhelming majority of state legislatures have drawn a clear line between assisting suicide and withdrawing or permitting the refusal of unwanted lifesaving medical treatment by prohibiting the former and permitting the latter. And "nearly all states expressly disapprove of suicide and assisted suicide either in statutes dealing with durable powers of attorney in health-care situations, or in 'living will' statutes." Thus, even as the States move to protect and promote patients' dignity at the end of life, they remain opposed to physician-assisted suicide.

New York is a case in point. The State enacted its current assisted-suicide statutes in 1965. Since then, New York has acted several times to protect patients' common-law [that established by usage and tradition] right to refuse treatment. In so doing, however, the State has neither endorsed a general right to "hasten death" nor approved physician-assisted suicide. Quite the opposite: The State has reaffirmed the line between "killing" and "letting die." More recently, the New York State Task Force on Life and the Law studied assisted suicide and euthanasia and, in 1994, unanimously recommended against legalization. In the Task Force's view, "allowing decisions to forego life-sustaining treatment and allowing assisted suicide or euthanasia have radically different consequences and meanings for public policy."

This Court has also recognized, at least implicitly, the distinction between letting a patient die and making that patient die. In *Cruzan v. Director, Missouri Department of Health,* we concluded that "[t]he principle that a competent person has a constitutionally protected liberty interest in refusing unwanted medical treatment may be inferred from our prior decisions," and we assumed the existence of such a right for purposes of that case. But our assumption of a right to refuse treatment was grounded not, as the Court of Appeals supposed, on the proposition that patients have a general and abstract "right to hasten death," but on well established, traditional rights to bodily integrity and freedom from unwanted touching. In fact, we observed that "the majority of States in this country have laws imposing criminal penalties on one who assists another to commit suicide." *Cruzan* therefore provides no support for the notion that refusing life-sustaining medical treatment is "nothing more nor less than suicide."

For all these reasons, we disagree with respondents' claim that the distinction between refusing lifesaving medical treatment and assisted suicide is "arbitrary" and "irrational." Granted, in some cases, the line between the two may not be clear, but certainty is not required, even were it possible. Logic and contemporary practice support New York's judgment that the two acts are different, and New York may therefore, consistent with the Constitution, treat them differently. By permitting everyone to refuse unwanted medical treatment while prohibiting anyone from assisting a suicide, New York law follows a longstanding and rational distinction.

New York's reasons for recognizing and acting on this distinction - including prohibiting intentional killing and preserving life, preventing suicide, maintaining physicians' role as their patients' healers, protecting vulnerable people from indifference, prejudice, and psychological and financial pressure to end their lives, and avoiding a possible slide towards euthanasia - are discussed in greater detail in our opinion in *Glucksberg*. These valid and important public interests easily satisfy the constitutional requirement that a legislative classification bear a rational relation to some legitimate end. The judgment of the Court of Appeals is reversed.

The Presidential Line Item Veto
A Challenge To A New Presidential Power
President William J. Clinton v. The City of New York

Every Bill which shall have passed the House of Representatives and the Senate, shall before it becomes a Law, be presented to the President of the United States.   - The Constitution's Presentment Clause

Under the United States Constitution's Presentment Clause (Article I, Section 7, Clause 2), three steps are required for a bill to becomes a law. The *exact same text of the bill* must be approved by a majority of: (1) the House, and (2) the Senate, before being (3) presented to the President of the United States for either his approval or his veto. A Presidential veto, unless overridden by a two-thirds majority of Congress, nullifies the *entire* bill.

The Presidential Line Item Veto Act became effective on January 1, 1997. The purpose of the Act was to allow the President of the United States, after a majority in the House and Senate had approved *the exact same text of a bill*, to veto specific spending items within a bill without nullifying the entire bill.

On August 11, 1997 President Clinton used the line item veto power for the first time - once to nullify a provision of the Balanced Budget Act of 1997, giving New York City a tax break, and again to nullify a provision of the Taxpayer Relief Act of 1997, giving Idaho farmers a tax benefit. The New York City Health and Hospitals Corporation and the Snake River (Idaho) Potato Grower Cooperative filed actions against the President challenging the constitutionality of the Line Item Veto Act.

The U.S. District Court, which consolidated the two cases, found the Line Item Veto Act to be unconstitutional. In effect the Court found the Act authorized the President to create a law different from *the exact same text of the bill* approved by the Congress. The President appealed to the United States Supreme Court.

On June 25, 1998 the 6-3 decision of the United States Supreme Court was announced by Justice John Paul Stevens.

The *Presidential Line Item Veto* Court

Chief Justice William Rehnquist
Appointed Chief Justice by President Reagan
Appointed Associate Justice by President Nixon
Served 1971 -

Associate Justice John Paul Stevens
Appointed by President Ford
Served 1975 -

Associate Justice Sandra Day O'Connor
Appointed by President Reagan
Served 1981 -

Associate Justice Antonin Scalia
Appointed by President Reagan
Served 1986 -

Associate Justice Anthony Kennedy
Appointed by President Reagan
Served 1988 -

Associate Justice David Souter
Appointed by President Bush
Served 1990 -

Associate Justice Clarence Thomas
Appointed by President Bush
Served 1991 -

Associate Justice Ruth Bader Ginsberg
Appointed by President Clinton
Served 1993 -

Associate Justice Stephen Breyer
Appointed by President Clinton
Served 1994 -

The unedited legal text of *President William J. Clinton v. The City of New York* can be found in volume 524 of *United States Reports*. Our edited plain-English text follows.

President William J. Clinton
v.
The City of New York
June 25, 1998

Justice John Paul Stevens: The Line Item Veto Act was enacted in April 1996 and became effective on January 1, 1997. . . .

[T]he President exercised his authority to cancel [selected provisions] in the Balanced Budget Act of 1997 and . . . in the Taxpayer Relief Act of 1997. [The New York City Health and Hospitals Corporation and the Snake River (Idaho) Potato Grower Cooperative], claiming that they had been injured by . . . those cancellations, filed these cases [now consolidated] in the District Court. That Court . . . held the statute invalid and we . . . expedited our review. We now hold . . . that the cancellation procedures set forth in [the Line Item Veto] Act violate the Presentment Clause, Article 1, Section 7, Clause 2, of the Constitution.

. . . . [T]he District Court held that the cancellations did not conform to the constitutionally mandated procedures for the enactment or repeal of laws in two respects. First, the laws that resulted after the cancellations "were different from those consented to by both Houses of Congress." Moreover, the President violated Article I "when he unilaterally cancelled provisions of duly enacted statutes." As a separate basis for its decision, the District Court also held that the Act "impermissibly disrupts the balance of powers among the three branches of government."

. . . . The Line Item Veto Act gives the President the power to "cancel in whole" three types of provisions that have been signed into law: "(1) any dollar amount of discretionary budget authority; (2) any item of new direct spending; or (3) any limited tax benefit." It is undisputed that the

New York case involves an "item of new direct spending" and that the Snake River case involves a "limited tax benefit" as those terms are defined in the Act. It is also undisputed that each of those provisions had been signed into law pursuant to Article I, Section 7, of the Constitution before it was cancelled.

The Act requires the President to adhere to precise procedures whenever he exercises his cancellation authority. In identifying items for cancellation he must consider the legislative history, the purposes, and other relevant information about the items. He must determine, with respect to each cancellation, that it will "(i) reduce the Federal budget deficit; (ii) not impair any essential Government functions; and (iii) not harm the national interest." Moreover, he must transmit a special message to Congress notifying it of each cancellation within five calendar days (excluding Sundays) after the enactment of the cancelled provision. It is undisputed that the President meticulously followed these procedures in these cases.

A cancellation takes effect upon receipt by Congress of the special message from the President. If, however, a "disapproval bill" pertaining to a special message is enacted into law, the cancellations set forth in that message become "null and void." The [Line Item Veto] Act sets forth a detailed expedited procedure for the consideration of a "disapproval bill," but no such bill was passed for either of the cancellations involved in these cases. A majority vote of both Houses is sufficient to enact a disapproval bill. The [Line Item Veto] Act does not grant the President the authority to cancel a disapproval bill, but he does, of course, retain his constitutional authority to veto such a bill.

The effect of a cancellation is plainly stated in [the Line Item Veto Act], which defines the principal terms used in the Act. With respect to both an item of new direct spending and a limited tax benefit, the cancellation prevents the item "from having legal force or effect." Thus, under the plain text of the statute, the two actions of the President that are challenged in these cases prevented one section of the Balanced Budget Act of 1997 and one section of the Taxpayer Relief Act of 1997 "from having legal force or effect." The remaining provisions of those statutes, with the exception of the second cancelled item in the latter, continue to have the same force and effect as they had when signed into law.

In both legal and practical effect, the President has amended two Acts of Congress by repealing a portion of each. "[R]epeal of statutes, no less than enactment, must conform with Article I." There is no provision in the Constitution that authorizes the President to enact, to amend, or to repeal statutes. Both Article I and Article II assign responsibilities to the President that directly relate to the lawmaking process, but neither addresses the issue presented by these cases. The President "shall from time to time give to the Congress information on the State of the Union, and recommend to their consideration such measures as he shall judge necessary and expedient. . . ." Thus, he may initiate and influence legislative proposals. Moreover, after a bill has passed both Houses of Congress, but "before it become[s] a law," it must be presented to the President. If he approves it, "he shall sign it, but if not he shall return it, with his objections to that House in which it shall have originated, who shall enter the objections at large on their journal, and proceed to reconsider it." His "return" of a bill, which is usually described as a "veto" is subject to being overridden by a two-thirds vote in each House.

There are important differences between the President's "return" of a bill pursuant to Article I, Section 7, and the exercise of the President's cancellation authority pursuant to the Line Item Veto Act. The constitutional return takes place before the bill becomes law; the statutory cancellation occurs after the bill becomes law. The constitutional return is of the entire bill; the statutory cancellation is of only a part. Although the Constitution expressly authorizes the President to play a role in the process of enacting statutes, it is silent on the subject of unilateral Presidential action that either repeals or amends parts of duly enacted statutes.

There are powerful reasons for construing [interpreting] constitutional silence on this profoundly important issue as equivalent to an express prohibition. The procedures governing the enactment of statutes set forth in the text of Article I were the product of the great debates and compromises that produced the Constitution itself. Familiar historical materials provide abundant support for the conclusion that the power to enact statutes may only "be exercised in accord with a single, finely wrought and exhaustively considered, procedure." Our first President understood the text of the Presentment Clause as requiring that he either "approve all the parts of a bill, or reject it in toto." What has emerged in these cases from the President's exercise of his statutory cancellation powers, however, are truncated versions of two bills that passed both Houses of Congress. They are not the product of the "finely wrought" procedure that the Framers designed.

. . . [T]he Government suggested that the cancellations at issue in these cases do not effect a "repeal" of the cancelled items because under the special "lockbox provisions of the Act, a cancelled item "retain[s] real, legal budgetary effect" insofar as it prevents Congress and the President from spending the savings that result from the cancellation. The text of the Act expressly provides, however, that a cancellation prevents a direct spending or tax benefit provision "from having legal force or effect." That a cancelled item may have "real, legal budgetary effect" as a result of the lockbox procedure does not change the fact that by cancelling the items at issue in these cases, the President made them entirely inoperative as to [New York City and the Snake River Cooperative]. [The vetoed provision] of the Taxpayer Relief Act no longer provides a tax benefit, and [the vetoed provision] of the Balanced Budget Act of 1997 no longer relieves New York of its [tax] liability. Such significant changes do not lose their character simply because the cancelled provisions may have some continuing financial effect on the Government. The cancellation of one section of a statute may be the functional equivalent of a partial repeal even if a portion of the section is not cancelled.

. . . . Neither are we persuaded by the Government's contention that the President's authority to cancel new direct spending and tax benefit items is no greater than his traditional authority to decline to spend appropriated funds. The Government has reviewed in some detail the series of statutes in which Congress has given the Executive broad discretion over the expenditure of appropriated funds. For example, the First Congress appropriated "sum[s] not exceeding" specified amounts to be spent on various Government operations. In those statutes, as in later years, the President was given wide discretion with respect to both the amounts to be spent and how the money would be allocated among different functions. It is argued that the Line Item Veto Act merely confers comparable discretionary authority over the expenditure of appropriated funds. The critical difference between this statute and all of its predecessors, however, is that unlike any of them, this Act gives the President the unilateral power to change the text of duly enacted statutes. None of the Act's predecessors could even arguably have been construed to authorize such a change.

Although they are implicit in what we have already written, the profound importance of these cases makes it appropriate to emphasize three points.

First, we express no opinion about the wisdom of the procedures authorized by the Line Item Veto Act. Many members of both major political parties who have served in the Legislative and the Executive Branches have long advocated the enactment of such procedures for the purpose of "ensur[ing] greater fiscal accountability in Washington." The text of the Act was itself the product of much debate and deliberation in both Houses of Congress and that precise text was signed into law by the President. We do not lightly conclude that their action was unauthorized by the Constitution. We have, however, twice had full argument and briefing on the question and have concluded that our duty is clear.

Second, although [the City of New York and the Snake River Cooperative] challenge the validity of the Act on alternative grounds, the only issue we address concerns the "finely wrought" procedure commanded by the Constitution. We have been favored with extensive debate about the scope of Congress' power to delegate law-making authority, or its functional equivalent, to the President. The excellent briefs [written statements to the court] filed by the parties and their amici curiae [friends of the Court] have provided us with valuable historical information that illuminates the delegation issue but does not really bear on the narrow issue that is dispositive of [effecting] these cases. Thus, because we conclude that the Act's cancellation provisions violate Article I, Section 7, of the Constitution, we find it unnecessary to consider the District Court's alternative holding that the Act "impermissibly disrupts the balance of powers among the three branches of government."

Third, our decision rests on the narrow ground that the procedures authorized by the Line Item Veto Act are not authorized by the Constitution. The Balanced Budget Act of 1997 is a 500-page document that became [a Public Law] after three procedural steps were taken:

(1) a bill containing its exact text was approved by a majority of the Members of the House of Representatives;
(2) the Senate approved precisely the same text; and
(3) that text was signed into law by the President.

The Constitution explicitly requires that each of those three steps be taken before a bill may "become a law." If one paragraph of that text had been omitted at any one of those three stages, [the] Public Law would not have been validly enacted. If the Line Item Veto Act were valid, it would authorize the President to create a different law - one whose text was not voted on by either House of Congress or presented to the President for signature. Something that might be known as [the "Public Law] as modified by the President" may or may not be desirable, but it is surely not a document that may "become a law" pursuant to the procedures designed by the Framers of Article I, Section 7, of the Constitution.

If there is to be a new procedure in which the President will play a different role in determining the final text of what may "become a law," such change must come not by legislation but through the amendment procedures set forth in Article V of the Constitution.

The judgment of the District Court is affirmed [upheld].

The United States Constitution

PREAMBLE

We the people of the United States, in order to form a more perfect union, establish justice, insure domestic tranquility, provide for the common defense, promote the general welfare, and secure the blessings of liberty to ourselves and our posterity, do ordain and establish this Constitution for the United States of America.

ARTICLE I

Section 1. All legislative powers herein granted shall be vested in a Congress of the United States, which shall consist of a Senate and House of Representatives.

Section 2. (1) The House of Representatives shall be composed of members chosen every second year by the people of several states, and the electors in each state shall have the qualifications requisite for electors of the most numerous branch of the State Legislature.

(2) No person shall be a Representative who shall not have attained to the age of twenty-five years, and been seven years a citizen of the United States, and who shall not, when elected, be an inhabitant of that state in which he shall be chosen.

(3) Representatives and direct taxes shall be apportioned among the several states which may be included within this union, according to their respective numbers, which shall be determined by adding to the whole number of free persons, including those bound to service for a term of years, and excluding Indians not taxed, three-fifths of all other persons. The actual enumeration shall be made within three years after the first meeting of the Congress of the United

States, and within every subsequent term of ten years, in such manner as they shall by law direct. The number of Representatives shall not exceed one for every thirty thousand, but each state shall have at least one Representative; and until such enumeration shall be made, the State of New Hampshire shall be entitled to choose three, Massachusetts eight, Rhode Island and Providence Plantations one, Connecticut five, New York six, New Jersey four, Pennsylvania eight, Delaware one, Maryland six, Virginia ten, North Carolina five, South Carolina five, and Georgia three.

(4) When vacancies happen in the representation from any state, the executive authority thereof shall issue Writs of Election to fill such vacancies.

(5) The House of Representatives shall choose their Speaker and other Officers; and shall have the sole power of impeachment.

Section 3. (1) The Senate of the United States shall be composed of two Senators from each state, chosen by the legislature thereof, for six years; and each Senator shall have one vote.

(2) Immediately after they shall be assembled in consequence of the first election, they shall be divided as equally as may be into three classes. The seats of the Senators of the first class shall be vacated at the expiration of the second year, of the second class at the expiration of the fourth year, and of the third class at the expiration of the sixth year, so that one-third may be chosen every second year; and if vacancies happen by resignation, or otherwise, during the recess of the legislature of any state, the executive thereof may make temporary appointments until the next meeting of the legislature, which shall then fill such vacancies.

(3) No person shall be a Senator who shall not have attained to the age of thirty years, and been nine years a citizen of the United States, and who shall not, when elected, be an inhabitant of that state for which he shall be chosen.

(4) The Vice President of the United States shall be President of the Senate, but shall have no vote, unless they be equally divided.

(5) The Senate shall choose their other Officers, and also a President pro tempore, in the absence of the Vice President, or when he shall exercise the Office of President of the United States.

(6) The Senate shall have the sole power to try all impeachments. When sitting for that purpose, they shall be on oath or affirmation. When the President of the United States is tried, the Chief Justice shall preside: and no person shall be convicted without the concurrence of two-thirds of the members present.

(7) Judgment in cases of impeachment shall not extend further than to removal from office, and disqualification to hold and enjoy any office of honor, trust, or profit under the United States: but the party convicted shall nevertheless be liable and subject to indictment, trial, judgment, and punishment, according to law.

Section 4. (1) The times, places and manner of holding elections for Senators and Representatives, shall be prescribed in each state by the legislature thereof; but the Congress may at any time by law make or alter such regulations, except as to the places of choosing Senators.

(2) The Congress shall assemble at least once in every year, and such meeting shall be on the first Monday in December, unless they shall by law appoint a different day.

Section 5. (1) Each House shall be the judge of the elections, returns, and qualifications of its own members, and a majority of each shall constitute a quorum to do business; but a smaller number may adjourn from day to day, and may be authorized to compel the attendance of absent members, in such manner, and under such penalties as each House may provide.

(2) Each House may determine the rules of its proceedings, punish its members for disorderly behavior, and, with the concurrence of two-thirds, expel a member.

(3) Each House shall keep a journal of its proceedings, and from time to time publish the same, excepting such parts as may in their judgment require secrecy; and the yeas and nays of the members of either House on any question shall, at the desire of one-fifth of those present, be entered on the journal.

(4) Neither House, during the Session of Congress, shall, without the consent of the other, adjourn for more than three days, nor to any other place than that in which the two Houses shall be sitting.

Section 6. (1) The Senators and Representatives shall receive a compensation for their services, to be ascertained by law, and paid out of the Treasury of the United States. They shall in all cases, except treason, felony and breach of the peace, be privileged from arrest during their attendance at the session of their respective Houses, and in going to and returning from the same; and for any speech or debate in either House, they shall not be questioned in any other place.

(2) No Senator or Representative shall, during the time for which he was elected, be appointed to any civil office under the authority of the United States, which shall have been

created, or the emoluments whereof shall have been increased during such time and no person holding any office under the United States, shall be a member of either House during his continuance in office.

Section 7. (1) All bills for raising revenue shall originate in the House of Representatives; but the Senate may propose or concur with amendments as on other bills.

(2) Every bill which shall have passed the House of Representatives and the Senate, shall, before it become a law, be presented to the President of the United States; if he approve he shall sign it, but if not he shall return it, with his objections to the House in which it shall have originated, who shall enter the objections at large on their journal, and proceed to reconsider it. If after such reconsideration two-thirds of that House shall agree to pass the bill, it shall be sent together with the objections, to the other House, by which it shall likewise be reconsidered, and if approved by two-thirds of that House, it shall become a law. But in all such cases the votes of both Houses shall be determined by yeas and nays, and the names of the persons voting for and against the bill shall be entered on the journal of each House respectively. If any bill shall not be returned by the President within ten days (Sundays excepted) after it shall have been presented to him, the same shall be a law, in like manner as if he had signed it, unless the Congress by their adjournment prevent its return in which case it shall not be a law.

(3) Every order, resolution, or vote, to which the concurrence of the Senate and House of Representatives may be necessary (except on a question of adjournment) shall be presented to the President of the United States; and before the same shall take effect, shall be approved by him, or being disapproved by him, shall be repassed by two-thirds of

the Senate and House of Representatives, according to the rules and limitations prescribed in the case of a bill.

Section 8. (1) The Congress shall have the power to lay and collect taxes, duties, imposts and excises, to pay the debts and provide for the common defense and general welfare of the United States; but all duties, imposts and excises shall be uniform throughout the United States;

(2) To borrow money on the credit of the United States;

(3) To regulate commerce with foreign nations, and among the several states, and with the Indian Tribes;

(4) To establish an uniform Rule of Naturalization, and uniform laws on the subject of bankruptcies throughout the United States;

(5) To coin money, regulate the value thereof, and of foreign coin, and fix the standard of weights and measures;

(6) To provide for the punishment of counterfeiting the securities and current coin of the United States;

(7) To establish Post Offices and Post Roads;

(8) To promote the progress of science and useful arts, by securing for limited times to authors and inventors the exclusive right to their respective writings and discoveries;

(9) To constitute tribunals inferior to the Supreme Court;

(10) To define and punish piracies and felonies committed on the high seas, and offenses against the Law of Nations;

(11) To declare war, grant Letters of Marque and Reprisal, and make rules concerning captures on land and water;

(12) To raise and support armies, but no appropriation of money to that use shall be for a longer term than two years;

(13) To provide and maintain a Navy;

(14) To make rules for the government and regulation of the land and naval forces;

(15) To provide for calling forth the Militia to execute the laws of the Union, suppress insurrections and repel invasions;

(16) To provide for organizing, arming, and disciplining, the Militia, and for governing such part of them as may be employed in the service of the United States, reserving to the states respectively, the appointment of the Officers, and the authority of training the Militia according to the discipline prescribed by Congress;

(17) To exercise exclusive legislation in all cases whatsoever, over such district (not exceeding ten miles square) as may, by cession of particular states, and the acceptance of Congress, become the Seat of the Government of the United States, and to exercise like authority over all places purchased by the consent of the legislature of the state in which the same shall be, for the erection of forts, magazines, arsenals, dockyards, and other needful buildings; and

(18) To make all laws which shall be necessary and proper for carrying into execution the foregoing powers, and all other powers vested by this Constitution in the Government of the United States, or in any Department or Officer thereof.

Section 9. (1) The migration or importation of such persons as any of the states now existing shall think proper to admit, shall not be prohibited by the Congress prior to the year one thousand eight hundred and eight, but a tax or duty may be imposed on such importation, not exceeding ten dollars for each person.

(2) The privilege of the Writ of Habeas Corpus shall not be suspended, unless when in cases of rebellion or invasion the public safety may require it.

(3) No Bill of Attainder or ex post facto law shall be passed.

(4) No capitation, or other direct, tax shall be laid, unless in proportion to the Census or enumeration herein before directed to be taken.

(5) No tax or duty shall be laid on articles exported from any state.

(6) No preference shall be given by any regulation of commerce or revenue to the ports of one state over those of another: nor shall vessels bound to, or from, one state be obliged to enter, clear, or pay duties in another.

(7) No money shall be drawn from the Treasury, but in consequence of appropriations made by law; and a regular statement and account of the receipts and expenditures of all public money shall be published from time to time.

(8) No title of nobility shall be granted by the United States: and no person holding any office of profit or trust under them, shall, without the consent of the Congress, accept of any present, emolument, office, or title, of any kind whatever, from any King, Prince, or foreign State.

Section 10. (1) No state shall enter into any treaty, alliance, or confederation; grant Letter of Marque and Reprisal; coin money; emit bills of credit; make any thing but gold and silver coin a tender in payment of debts; pass any Bill of

Attainder, ex post facto law, or law impairing the obligation of contracts, or grant any title of nobility.

(2) No state shall, without the consent of the Congress, lay any imposts or duties on imports or exports, except what may be absolutely necessary for executing its inspection laws: and the net produce of all duties and imposts, laid by any state on imports or exports, shall be for the use of the Treasury of the United States; and all such laws shall be subject to the revision and control of the Congress.

(3) No state shall, without the consent of Congress, lay any duty of tonnage, keep troops, or ships of war in time of peace, enter into any agreement or compact with another state, or with a foreign power, or engage in war, unless actually invaded, or in such imminent danger as will not admit of delay.

ARTICLE II

Section 1. (1) The executive power shall be vested in a President of the United States of America. He shall hold his office during the term of four years, and, together with the Vice President, chosen for the same term, be elected, as follows:

(2) Each state shall appoint, in such manner as the legislature thereof may direct, a number of electors, equal to the whole number of Senators and Representatives to which the state may be entitled in the Congress; but no Senator or Representative, or person holding an office of trust or profit under the United States, shall be appointed an Elector.

(3) The Electors shall meet in their respective states, and vote by ballot for two persons, of whom one at least shall not be an inhabitant of the same state with themselves.

And they shall make a list of all the persons voted for, and of the number of votes for each; which list they shall sign and certify, and transmit sealed to the Seat of the Government of the United States, directed to the President of the Senate. The President of the Senate shall, in the presence of the Senate and House of Representatives, open all the certificates, and the votes shall then be counted. The person having the greatest number of votes shall be the President, if such number be a majority of the whole number of Electors appointed; and if there be more than one who have such majority, and have an equal number of votes, then the House of Representatives shall immediately choose by ballot one of them for President; and if no person have a majority, then from the five highest on the list the said House shall in like manner choose the President. But in choosing the President, the votes shall be taken by states the representation from each state having one vote; a quorum for this purpose shall consist of a member or members from two-thirds of the states, and a majority of all the states shall be necessary to a choice. In every case, after the choice of the President, the person having the greater number of votes of the Electors shall be the Vice President. But if there should remain two or more who have equal votes, the Senate shall choose from them by ballot the Vice President.

(4) The Congress may determine the time of choosing the Electors, and the day on which they shall give their votes; which day shall be the same throughout the United States.

(5) No person except a natural born citizen, or a citizen of the United States, at the time of the adoption of this Constitution, shall be eligible to the Office of President; neither shall any person be eligible to that Office who shall not have attained to the age of thirty-five years, and been fourteen years a resident within the United States.

(6) In case of the removal of the President from Office, or of his death, resignation or inability to discharge the powers and duties of the said Office, the same shall devolve on the Vice President, and the Congress may by law provide for the case of removal, death, resignation, or inability, both of the President and Vice President, declaring what Officer shall then act as President, and such Officer shall act accordingly, until the disability be removed, or a President shall be elected.

(7) The President shall, at stated times, receive for his services, a compensation, which shall neither be increased nor diminished during the period for which he shall have been elected, and he shall not receive within that period any other emolument from the United States, or any of them.

(8) Before he enter on the execution of his Office, he shall take the following Oath or Affirmation: "I do solemnly swear (or affirm) that I will faithfully execute the Office of President of the United States, and will to the best of my ability, preserve, protect and defend the Constitution of the United States."

Section 2. (1) The President shall be Commander in Chief of the Army and Navy of the United States, and of the militia of the several states, when called into the actual service of the United States; he may require the opinion, in writing, of the principal Officer in each of the Executive Departments, upon any subject relating to the duties of their respective Offices, and he shall have power to grant reprieves and pardons for offenses against the United States, except in cases of impeachment.

(2) He shall have power, by and with the advice and consent of the Senate to make treaties, provided two-thirds of the Senators present concur; and he shall nominate, and by and with the advice and consent of the Senate, shall ap-

point Ambassadors, other public Ministers and Consuls, Judges of the Supreme Court, and all other Officers of the United States, whose appointments are not herein otherwise provided for, and which shall be established by law; but the Congress may by law vest the appointment of such inferior Officers, as they think proper, in the President alone, in the courts of law, or in the Heads of Departments.

(3) The President shall have power to fill up all vacancies that may happen during the recess of the Senate, by granting commissions which shall expire at the end of their next Session.

Section 3. He shall from time to time give to the Congress information of the State of the Union, and recommend to their consideration such measures as he shall judge necessary and expedient; he may, on extraordinary occasions, convene both Houses, or either of them, and in case of disagreement between them, with respect to the time of adjournment, he may adjourn them to such time as he shall think proper; he shall receive Ambassadors and other public Ministers; he shall take care that the laws be faithfully executed, and shall commission all the Officers of the United States.

Section 4. The President, Vice President and all civil Officers of the United States, shall be removed from office on impeachment for, and conviction of, treason, bribery, or other high crimes and misdemeanors.

ARTICLE III

Section 1. The judicial power of the United States, shall be vested in one Supreme Court, and in such inferior courts as the Congress may from time to time ordain and establish. The Judges, both of the supreme and inferior courts, shall hold their Offices during good behaviour, and shall, at stated times, receive for their services a compensation, which shall not be diminished during their continuance in office.

Section 2. (1) The judicial power shall extend to all cases, in law and equity, arising under this Constitution, the laws of the United States, and treaties made, or which shall be made, under their authority; to all cases affecting Ambassadors, other public Ministers and Consuls; to all cases of admiralty and maritime jurisdiction; to controversies to which the United States shall be a party; to controversies between two or more states; between a state and citizens of another state; between citizens of different states; between citizens of the same state claiming lands under the grants of different states, and between a state, or the citizens thereof, and foreign states, citizens or subjects.

(2) In all cases affecting Ambassadors, other public Ministers and Consuls, and those in which a state shall be a party, the Supreme Court shall have original jurisdiction. In all the other cases before mentioned, the Supreme Court shall have appellate jurisdiction, both as to law and fact, with such exceptions, and under such regulations as the Congress shall make.

(3) The trial of all crimes, except in cases of impeachment, shall be by jury; and such trial shall be held in the state where the said crimes shall have been committed; but when not committed within any state, the trial shall be at such place or places as the Congress may by law have directed.

Section 3. (1) Treason against the United States, shall consist only in levying war against them, or, in adhering to their enemies, giving them aid and comfort. No person shall be convicted of treason unless on the testimony of two witnesses to the same overt act, or on confession in open Court.

(2) The Congress shall have power to declare the punishment of treason, but no Attainder of Treason shall work corruption of blood, or forfeiture except during the life of the person attainted.

ARTICLE IV

Section 1. Full faith and credit shall be given in each state to the public acts, records, and judicial proceedings of every other state. And the Congress may by general laws prescribe the manner in which such acts, records and proceedings shall be proved, and the effect thereof.

Section 2. (1) The citizens of each state shall be entitled to all privileges and immunities of citizens in the several states.

(2) A person charged in any state with treason, felony, or other crime, who shall flee from justice, and be found in another state, shall on demand of the executive authority of the state from which he fled, be delivered up, to be removed to the state having jurisdiction of the crime.

(3) No person held to service or labour in one state, under the laws thereof, escaping into another, shall, in consequence of any law or regulation therein, be discharged from such service or labour, but shall be delivered up on claim of the party to whom such service or labour may be due.

Section 3. (1) New states may be admitted by the Congress into this Union; but no new state shall be formed or erected within the jurisdiction of any other state; nor any state be formed by the junction of two or more states, or parts of states, without the consent of the legislatures of the states concerned as well as of the Congress.

(2) The Congress shall have power to dispose of and make all needful rules and regulations respecting the territory or

other property belonging to the United States; and nothing in this Constitution shall be so construed as to prejudice any claims of the United States, or of any particular state.

Section 4. The United States shall guarantee to every state in this Union a Republican form of government, and shall protect each of them against invasion; and on application of the Legislature, or of the Executive (when the Legislature cannot be convened) against domestic violence.

ARTICLE V

The Congress, whenever two-thirds of both Houses shall deem it necessary, shall propose amendments to this Constitution, or, on the application of the Legislatures of two-thirds of the several states, shall call a convention for proposing amendments, which, in either case, shall be valid to all intents and purposes, as part of this constitution, when ratified by the Legislatures of three-fourths of the several states, or by conventions in three-fourths thereof, as the one or the other mode of ratification may be proposed by the Congress; provided that no amendment which may be made prior to the year one thousand eight hundred and eight shall in any manner affect the first and fourth clauses in the Ninth Section of the first Article; and that no state, without its consent, shall be deprived of its equal suffrage in the Senate.

ARTICLE VI

(1) All debts contracted and engagements entered into, before the adoption of this Constitution shall be as valid against the United States under this Constitution, as under the Confederation.

(2) This Constitution, and the laws of the United States which shall be made in pursuance thereof; and all treaties

made, or which shall be made, under the authority of the United States, shall be the supreme law of the land; and the Judges in every state shall be bound thereby, any thing in the Constitution or laws of any state to the contrary notwithstanding.

(3) The Senators and Representatives before mentioned, and the Members of the several State Legislatures, and all executive and judicial Officers, both of the United States and of the several states, shall be bound by oath or affirmation, to support this Constitution; but no religious test shall ever be required as a qualification to any Office or public trust under the United States.

ARTICLE VII

The ratification of the Conventions of nine states shall be sufficient for the establishment of this Constitution between the states so ratifying the same.

AMENDMENT I (1791)

Congress shall make no law respecting an establishment of religion, or prohibiting the free exercise thereof; or abridging the freedom of speech, or of the press; or the right of the people peaceably to assemble, and to petition the Government for a redress of grievances.

AMENDMENT II (1791)

A well regulated Militia, being necessary to the security of a free State, the right of the people to keep and bear arms, shall not be infringed.

AMENDMENT III (1791)

No soldier shall, in time of peace be quartered in any house, without the consent of the owner, nor in time of war, but in a manner to be prescribed by law.

AMENDMENT IV (1791)

The right of the people to be secure in their persons, houses, papers, and effects, against unreasonable searches and seizures, shall not be violated, and no warrants shall issue, but upon probable cause, supported by oath or affirmation, and particularly describing the place to be searched, and the persons or things to be seized.

AMENDMENT V (1791)

No person shall be held to answer for a capital, or otherwise infamous crime, unless on a presentment or indictment of a Grand Jury, except in cases arising in the land or naval forces, or in the Militia, when in actual service in time of war or public danger; nor shall any person be subject for the same offense to be twice put in jeopardy of life or limb; nor shall be compelled in any criminal case to be a witness against himself, nor be deprived of life, liberty, or property, without due process of law; nor shall private property be taken for public use, without just compensation.

AMENDMENT VI (1791)

In all criminal prosecutions, the accused shall enjoy the right to a speedy and public trial, by an impartial jury of the state and district wherein the crime shall have been committed, which district shall have been previously ascertained by law, and to be informed of the nature and cause of the accusation; to be confronted with the witnesses against him; to have compulsory process for obtaining witnesses in his favor, and to have the assistance of counsel for his defense.

AMENDMENT VII (1791)

In suits at common law, where the value in controversy shall exceed twenty dollars, the right of trial by jury shall be preserved, and no fact tried by jury, shall be otherwise re-examined in any Court of the United States, than according to the rules of the common law.

AMENDMENT VIII (1791)

Excessive bail shall not be required, nor excessive fines imposed, nor cruel and unusual punishments inflicted.

AMENDMENT IX (1791)

The enumeration in the Constitution, of certain rights, shall not be construed to deny or disparage others retained by the people.

AMENDMENT X (1791)

The powers not delegated to the United States by the Constitution, nor prohibited by it to the States, are reserved to the States respectively, or to the people.

AMENDMENT XI (1798)

The judicial power of the United States shall not be construed to extend to any suit in law or equity, commenced or prosecuted against one of the United States by citizens of another state, or by citizens or subjects of any foreign state.

AMENDMENT XII (1804)

The Electors shall meet in their respective states and vote by ballot for President and Vice-President, one of whom, at least, shall not be an inhabitant of the same state with themselves; they shall name in their ballots the person voted for as President, and in distinct ballots the person voted for as Vice-President, and they shall make distinct lists of all persons voted for as President, and of all persons voted for as Vice-President, and of the number of votes for each, which lists they shall sign and certify, and transmit sealed to the seat of the government of the United States, directed to the President of the Senate; the President of the Senate shall, in the presence of the Senate and House of Representatives, open all the certificates and the votes shall then be counted; the person having the greatest number of votes for President, shall be the President, if such number be a majority of the persons having the highest numbers not exceeding three on the list of those voted for as President, the House of Representatives shall choose immediately, by ballot, the President. But in choosing the President, the votes shall be taken by states, the representation from each state having one vote; a quorum for this purpose shall consist of a member or members from two-thirds of the states, and a majority of all the states shall be necessary to a choice. And if the House of Representatives shall not choose a President whenever the right of choice shall devolve upon them before the fourth day of March next following, then the Vice-President shall act as President, as in the case of the death or other constitutional disability of the President. The person having the greatest number of votes as Vice-President, shall be the Vice-President, if such number be a majority of the whole number of Electors appointed, and if no person have a majority, then from the two highest numbers on the list, the Senate shall choose the Vice-President; a quorum for the purpose shall consist of two-thirds of the whole number of Senators, and a majority of the whole number shall be necessary to a choice. But no person constitutionally ineligible to the office of President shall be eligible to that of Vice-President of the United States.

AMENDMENT XIII (1865)

Section 1. Neither slavery nor involuntary servitude, except as a punishment for crime whereof the party shall have been duly convicted, shall exist within the United States, or any place subject to their jurisdiction.

Section 2. Congress shall have power to enforce this article by appropriate legislation.

AMENDMENT XIV (1868)

Section 1. All persons born or naturalized in the United States, and subject to the jurisdiction thereof, are citizens of the United States and of the state wherein they reside. No state shall make or enforce any law which shall abridge the privileges or immunities of citizens of the United States; nor shall any state deprive any person of life, liberty, or property, without due process of law; nor deny to any person within its jurisdiction the equal protection of the laws.

Section 2. Representatives shall be apportioned among the several states according to their respective numbers, counting the whole number of persons in each State excluding Indians not taxed. But when the right to vote at any election for the choice of electors for President and Vice President of the United States, Representatives in Congress, the Executive and Judicial officers of a state, or the members of the Legislature thereof, is denied to any of the male inhabitants of such state, being twenty-one years of age, and citizens of the United States, or in any way abridged, except for participation in rebellion, or other crime, the basis of representation therein shall be reduced in the proportion which the number of such male citizens shall bear to the whole number of male citizens twenty-one years of age in such state.

Section 3. No person shall be a Senator or Representative in Congress, or elector of President and Vice President, or hold any office, civil or military, under the United States, or under any state, who having previously taken an oath, as a member of Congress, or as an officer of the United States, or as a member of any state legislature, or as an executive or judicial officer of any state, to support the Constitution of the United States, shall have engaged in insurrection or rebellion against the same, or given aid or comfort to the enemies thereof. But Congress may by a vote of two-thirds of each House, remove such disability.

Section 4. The validity of the public debt of the United States, authorized by law, including debts incurred for payment of pensions and bounties for services in suppressing insurrection or rebellion, shall not be questioned. But neither the United States nor any state shall assume or pay any debt or obligation incurred in aid of insurrection or rebellion against the United States, or any claim for the loss or emancipation of any slave; but all such debts, obligations and claims shall be held illegal and void.

Section 5. The Congress shall have power to enforce, by appropriate legislation, the provisions of this article.

AMENDMENT XV (1870)

Section 1. The right of citizens of the United States to vote shall not be denied or abridged by the United States or by any state on account of race, color, or previous condition of servitude.

Section 2. The Congress shall have power to enforce this article by appropriate legislation.

AMENDMENT XVI (1913)

The Congress shall have power to lay and collect taxes on income, from whatever source derived, without apportionment among the several states, and without regard to any census or enumeration.

AMENDMENT XVII (1913)

(1) The Senate of the United States shall be composed of two Senators from each state, elected by the people thereof, for six years; and each Senator shall have one vote. The electors in each State shall have the qualifications requisite for electors of the most numerous branch of the state legislatures.

(2) When vacancies happen in the representation of any state in the Senate, the executive authority of such state shall issue writs of election to fill such vacancies: provided, that the legislature of any state may empower the executive thereof to make temporary appointments until the people fill the vacancies by election as the legislature may direct.

(3) This amendment shall not be so construed as to affect the election or term of any Senator chosen before it becomes valid as part of the Constitution.

AMENDMENT XVIII (1919)

Section 1. After one year from the ratification of this article the manufacture, sale, or transportation of intoxicating liquors within, the importation thereof into, or the exportation thereof from the United States and all territory subject to the jurisdiction thereof for beverage purposes is hereby prohibited.

Section 2. The Congress and the several states shall have concurrent power to enforce this article by appropriate legislation.

Section 3. This article shall be inoperative unless it shall have been ratified as an amendment to the Constitution by the legislatures of the several states, as provided in the Constitution, within seven years from the date of the submission hereof to the states by the Congress.

AMENDMENT XIX (1920)

(1) The right of citizens of the United States to vote shall not be denied or abridged by the United States or by any state on account of sex.

(2) Congress shall have power to enforce this article by appropriate legislation.

AMENDMENT XX (1933)

Section 1. The terms of the President and Vice President shall end at noon on the 20th day of January, and the terms of Senators and Representatives at noon on the 3d day of January, of the years in which such terms would have ended if this article had not been ratified; and the terms of their successors shall then begin.

Section 2. The Congress shall assemble at least once in every year, and such meeting shall begin at noon on the 3d day of January, unless they shall by law appoint a different day.

Section 3. If, at the time fixed for the beginning of the term of the President, the President elect shall have died, the Vice President elect shall become President. If the President shall not have been chosen before the time fixed for the beginning of his term, or if the President elect shall have failed to qualify, then the Vice President elect shall act as President until a President shall have qualified; and the Congress may by law provide for the case wherein neither a President elect nor a Vice President elect shall have qualified, declaring who shall then act as President, or the manner in which one who is to act shall be selected, and such person shall act accordingly until a President or Vice President shall have qualified.

Section 4. The Congress may by law provide for the case of the death of any of the persons from whom the House of Representatives may choose a President whenever the right of choice shall have devolved upon them, and for the case of the death of any of the persons from whom the Senate may choose a Vice President whenever the right of choice shall have devolved upon them.

Section 5. Sections 1 and 2 shall take effect on the 15th day of October following the ratification of this article.

Section 6. This article shall be inoperative unless it shall have been ratified as an amendment to the Constitution by the legislatures of three-fourths of the several states within seven years from the date of its submission.

AMENDMENT XXI (1933)

Section 1. The eighteenth article of amendment to the Constitution of the United States is hereby repealed.

Section 2. The transportation or importation into any state, territory, or possession of the United States for delivery or use therein of intoxicating liquors, in violation of the laws thereof, is hereby prohibited.

Section 3. This article shall be inoperative unless it shall have been ratified as an amendment to the Constitution by conventions in the several states, as provided in the Constitution, within seven years from the date of the submission hereof to the states by the Congress.

AMENDMENT XXII (1951)

Section 1. No person shall be elected to the office of the President more than twice, and no person who has held the office of President, or acted as President, for more than two years of a term to which some other person was elected President shall be elected to the office of President more than once. But this Article shall not apply to any person holding the office of President when this Article was proposed by the Congress, and shall not prevent any person who may be holding the office of President, or acting as President, during the term within which this Article becomes operative from holding the office of President or acting as President during the remainder of such term.

Section 2. This article shall be inoperative unless it shall have been ratified as an amendment to the Constitution by the legislatures of three-fourths of the several states within seven years from the date of its submission to the states by the Congress.

AMENDMENT XXIII (1961)

Section 1. The District constituting the seat of Government of the United States shall appoint in such manner as the Congress may direct:

A number of electors of President and Vice President equal to the whole number of Senators and Representatives in Congress to which the District would be entitled if it were a state, but in no event more than the least populous state; they shall be in addition to those appointed by the states, but they shall be considered, for the purposes of the election of President and Vice President, to be electors appointed by a state; and they shall meet in the District and perform such duties as provided by the twelfth article of amendment.

Section 2. The Congress shall have power to enforce this article by appropriate legislation.

AMENDMENT XXIV (1964)

Section 1. The right of citizens of the United States to vote in any primary or other election for President or Vice President, for electors for President or Vice President, or for Senator or Representative in Congress, shall not be denied or abridged by the United States, or any state by reason of failure to pay any poll tax or other tax.

Section 2. The Congress shall have power to enforce this article by appropriate legislation.

AMENDMENT XXV (1967)

Section 1. In case of the removal of the President from office or of his death or resignation, the Vice President shall become President.

Section 2. Whenever there is a vacancy in the office of the Vice President, the President shall nominate a Vice President who shall take office upon confirmation by a majority vote of both Houses of Congress.

Section 3. Whenever the President transmits to the President pro tempore of the Senate and the Speaker of the House of Representatives his written declaration that he is unable to discharge the powers and duties of his office, and until he transmits to them a written declaration to the contrary, such powers and duties shall be discharged by the Vice President as Acting President.

Section 4. Whenever the Vice President and a majority of either the principal officers of the executive departments or of such other body as Congress may by law provide, transmit to the President pro tempore of the Senate and the Speaker of the House of Representatives their written declaration that the President is unable to discharge the powers and duties of his office, the Vice President shall immediately assume the powers and duties of the office as Acting President.

Thereafter, when the President transmits to the President pro tempore of the Senate and the Speaker of the House of Representatives his written declaration that no inability exists, he shall resume the powers and duties of his office unless the Vice President and a majority of either the principal officers of the executive department or of such other body as Congress may by law provide, transmit within four days to the President pro tempore of the Senate and the Speaker of the House of Representatives their written declaration that the President is unable to discharge the powers and duties of his office. Thereupon Congress shall decide the issue, assembling within forty-eight hours for that purpose if not in session. If the Congress, within twenty-one days after receipt of the latter written declaration, or, if Congress is not in session, within twenty-one days after Congress is required to assemble, determines by two-thirds vote of both Houses that the President is unable to discharge the power and duties of his office, the Vice President shall continue to discharge the same as Acting President; otherwise, the President shall resume the powers and duties of his office.

AMENDMENT XXVI (1971)

Section 1. The right of citizens of the United States, who are eighteen years of age or older, to vote shall not be denied or abridged by the United States or by any state on account of age.

Section 2. The Congress shall have power to enforce this article by appropriate legislation.

AMENDMENT XXVII (1992)

No law, varying the compensation for the services of the Senators and Representatives, shall take effect, until an election of Representatives shall have intervened.

Bibliography

The Aaron Burr Conspiracy

Abernethy, Thomas Perkins. *The Burr Conspiracy*. New York, NY: Oxford University Press, 1954.

Elliott, John Carroll. *Charged With Treason*. Parsons, WV: McClain Print. Co., 1986.

Mary-Jo Kline, Editor. *Political Correspondence and Public Papers of Aaron Burr*. Princeton, NJ: Princeton University Press, 1983.

Lomask, Milton. *Aaron Burr: The Conspiracy and Years of Exile, 1805-1836*. New York, NY: Farrar, Straus & Giroux, 1982.

Daniel Webster's Defense of Dartmouth College

Dickey, John Sloan. *Eleazar Wheelock, Daniel Webster, and Their Pioneer Dartmouth College*. New York, NY: Newcomen Society in North America, 1954.

Fuess, Claude Moore. *Daniel Webster*. Hamden, CT: Archon Books, 1963.

Sterling, John C. *Daniel Webster and a Small College*. Hanover, NH: Dartmouth Publications, 1965.

Women's Work

Brandeis, Louis Dembitz (assisted by Josephine Goldmark). *Women in Industry: Decision of the United States Supreme Court in Muller v. Oregon*. New York, NY: Reprinted for the National Consumers' League, 1908.

Woloch, Nancy. *Muller v. Oregon: A Brief History with Documents*. Boston, MA: St. Martin's Press, 1996.

The Right to Bear Arms

Cottrol, Robert J., Editor. *Gun Control and the Constitution: Sources and Explorations on the Second Amendment*. New York, NY: Garland Pub. Co., 1993.

Halbrook, Stephen P. *That Every Man Be Armed: The Evolution of a Constitutional Right*. Albuquerque, NM: University of New Mexico Press, 1984.

Hawxhurst, Joan C. *The Second Amendment*. Englewood Cliffs, NJ: Silver Burdett Press, 1991.

The "Sick Chicken" Case

Himmelberg, Robert F. *The Origins of the National Recovery Administration*. New York, NY: Fordham University Press, 1993.

Maidment, R.A. *The Judicial Response to the New Deal: The U.S. Supreme Court and Economic Regulation, 1934-1936*. New York, NY: Manchester University Press, 1991.

Mussatti, James. *New Deal Decisions of the United States Supreme Court*. Los Angeles, CA: California Publications, 1936.

The Law of War

Barker, A.J. *Yamashita*. New York, NY: Ballantine Books, 1973.

Lael, Richard L. *The Yamashita Precedent: War Crimes and Command Responsibility*. Wilmington, DE: Scholarly Resources, 1982.

Taylor, Lawrence. *A Trial of Generals: Homma, Yamashita, MacArthur.* South Bend, IN: Icarus Press, 1981.

Unamerican Activities

Fariello, Griffin. *Red Scare: Memories of the American Inquisition.* New York, NY: W.W. Norton & Co., 1995.

One Person, One Vote

Balinski, M. L., and H. Peyton Young. *Fair Representation: Meeting the Ideal of One Man, One Vote.* New Haven, CT: Yale University Press, 1982.

O'Rourke, Timothy G. *The Impact of Reapportionment.* New Brunswick, NJ: Transaction Books, 1980.

The Right to Die

Beauchamp, Tom L., et al. *Matters of Life and Death.* Philadelphia, PA: Temple University Press, 1980.

DeSimone, Cathleen. *Death on Demand: Physician-Assisted Suicide in the United States.* Buffalo, NY: W.S. Hein, 1996.

Harrison, Maureen, and Steve Gilbert, Editors. *Life, Death, and the Law: Landmark Right to Die Decisions.* San Diego, CA: Excellent Books, 1997.

Meisel, Alan. *The Right to Die.* New York, NY: John Wiley & Sons, 1995.

The Presidential Line Item Veto

The Joint Committee on Taxation. *Analysis of Provisions Contained in the Line Item Veto Act.* Washington, DC: U.S. Government Printing Office, 1997.

The Supreme Court

Agresto, John. *The Supreme Court and Constitutional Democracy.* Ithaca, NY: Cornell University Press, 1984.

Cox, Archibald. *The Court and the Constitution.* New York, NY: Houghton-Mifflin, 1988.

Dumbauld, Edward. *The Bill of Rights and What It Means Today.* New York, NY: Greenwood Press, 1979.

Goode, Stephen. *The Controversial Court: Supreme Court Influences on American Life.* New York, NY: Messner, 1982.

Lawson, Don. *Landmark Supreme Court Cases.* Hillside, NJ: Enslow Publishers, Inc., 1987.

Rehnquist, William H. *The Supreme Court: How It Was, How It Is.* New York, NY: Morrow, 1987.

Woodward, Bob, and Scott Armstrong. *The Brethren: Inside the Supreme Court.* New York, NY: Simon & Schuster, 1979.

Yudof, Mark. *When Government Speaks: Politics, Law, and Government Expression in America.* Berkeley, CA: University of California Press, 1983.

Index

Also Available From Excellent Books

LANDMARK DECISIONS OF THE UNITED STATES SUPREME COURT I

SCHOOL DESEGREGATION

OBSCENITY

SCHOOL PRAYER

FAIR TRIALS

SEXUAL PRIVACY

CENSORSHIP

ABORTION

AFFIRMATIVE ACTION

BOOK BANNING

FLAG BURNING

Also Available From Excellent Books

LANDMARK DECISIONS OF THE UNITED STATES SUPREME COURT III

EXECUTIVE PRIVILEGE

CLEAR AND PRESENT DANGER

FORCED STERILIZATION

MOB JUSTICE

THE PLEDGE OF ALLEGIANCE

ILLEGAL SEARCH & SEIZURE

INTERRACIAL MARRIAGE

MONKEY TRIALS

SEXUAL HARASSMENT

CHURCH AND STATE

EXCELLENT BOOKS ORDER FORM

(Please xerox this form so it will be available to other readers.)

Please send
Copy(ies)

_____ of LANDMARK DECISIONS I @ $16.95
_____ of LANDMARK DECISIONS II @ $16.95
_____ of LANDMARK DECISIONS III @ $16.95
_____ of LANDMARK DECISIONS IV @ $16.95
_____ of LANDMARK DECISIONS V @ $16.95
_____ of LANDMARK DECISIONS VI @ $16.95
_____ of SCHOOLHOUSE DECISIONS @ $16.95
_____ of LIFE, DEATH, AND THE LAW @ $16.95
_____ of FREEDOM OF SPEECH DECISIONS @ $16.95
_____ of FREEDOM OF THE PRESS DECISIONS @ $16.95
_____ of FREEDOM OF RELIGION DECISIONS @ $16.95
_____ of THE MURDER REFERENCE @ $16.95
_____ of THE RAPE REFERENCE @ $16.95
_____ of ABORTION DECISIONS: THE 1970's @ $16.95
_____ of ABORTION DECISIONS: THE 1980's @ $16.95
_____ of ABORTION DECISIONS: THE 1990's @ $16.95
_____ of CIVIL RIGHTS DECISIONS: 19th CENTURY @ $16.95
_____ of CIVIL RIGHTS DECISIONS: 20th CENTURY @ $16.95
_____ of THE ADA HANDBOOK @ $16.95

Name: _____

Address: _____

City: _____ State: _____ Zip: _____

Add $1 per book for shipping and handling.
California residents add sales tax.

OUR GUARANTEE: Any Excellent Book may be returned at
any time for any reason and a full refund will be made.

Mail your check or money order to: Excellent Books,
Post Office Box 131322, Carlsbad, California 92013-1322
or call/fax: (760) 598-5069 or e-mail us at: xlntbks@aol.com